Sustained for the Journey

Finding hope and freedom
after loss & life-threatening challenges.
Believing for the impossible.

by Jervae Brooks

TRILOGY

Sustained for the Journey

Trilogy Christian Publishers A Wholly Owned Subsidiary of Trinity Broadcasting Network

2442 Michelle Drive Tustin, CA 92780

Rights Department, 2442 Michelle Drive, Tustin, CA 92780.

Trilogy Christian Publishing/TBN and colophon are trademarks of Trinity Broadcasting Network.

Cover design by: Natalee Dunning

Back cover photo credit: Joan Bennett

For information about special discounts for bulk purchases, please contact Trilogy Christian Publishing.

Manufactured in the United States of America

10 9 8 7 6 5 4 3 2 1

Library of Congress Cataloging-in-Publication Data is available.

ISBN: 978-1-63769-606-4

E-ISBN: 978-1-63769-607-1

DEDICATION

This book is dedicated to all who feel they can't go on. The weight of your life seems too heavy, the pit of despair too deep, the silence of heaven too deafening. The battle is fierce, and you feel afraid.

I am here to tell you that yes, my friend, you can go on. Trust in God's ever-lasting love. He will give you the strength and courage to never give up!

> But You, O Lord, are a shield for me, My glory and the One who lifts up my head. I cried to the Lord with my voice, And He heard me from His holy hill. Selah. I lay down and slept; I awoke, for the Lord sustained me.
>
> Psalm 3:3-5 (NKJV)

Sustained (adj.): continuing for an extended period or without interruption.

THANK YOU

It is with a humble and thankful heart that I see my name printed on the front of this book as the author. Not only does my story include so many others who are intricately woven throughout the journey chronicled on these pages, but it is also surely a recording of my life's journey that I have not written alone.

Dwight, from the moment I met you that January evening in 1969, it has been an exciting and eventful journey. Most parts of our fifty-plus-year journey have been "no laughing matter," but we have managed to come through with our love and our senses of humor intact. I love you more every day and would not wish myself to go through this life with anyone but you. Your well-placed words of wisdom and encouragement have kept me going through the long process of writing these pages. Thank you for always believing I could do it.

Martha Stanley, ever since we first met at the headquarter offices of Aglow International in 2006, it seems we have had an innate understanding of one another. You are a brilliant word-smith, computer whiz, and deeply caring friend. Thank you for the hours you have spent reading and re-reading this manuscript for me, always offering valuable and wise suggestions.

To all the others—you know who you are—who have helped me find my voice in words, thank you. Your encouragement and belief that this story needs to be told have kept me going.

And of course—first, last, and all thanks—to my precious friend Jesus Christ. All honor to You for being the true Sustainer of my life.

Endorsements

"*Proverbs 31:26 speaks of the virtuous woman in this way: 'She opens her mouth with skillful and godly wisdom, and in her tongue is the law of kindness—giving counsel and instruction.'*

"*Jervae serves as Executive Director of the International Field for Aglow, and as such, she is in contact with and helps lead the Aglow leadership in the nations. She does so with skill, wisdom, and yet graciousness. She brings a measure of calm and safety as she confidently encourages them forward.*

"*As a friend and co-worker, I have witnessed Jervae's journey through many of the life-altering places spoken of in this book. Through these trials, Jervae has developed the godly wisdom, patience, and strength she shares with the nations she leads. I encourage you to absorb the godly wisdom contained in these pages. I love how God uses Jervae, and so will you.*"

—Jane Hansen Hoyt, CEO/International President
Aglow International

"*I just finished reading Jervae's story about her and her husband's life. It is a story of encouragement in the face of life's difficult challenges. Their faith in God shines through and will encourage you to have faith in God in your challenges. I have been Dwight and Jervae's pastor and friend for many years. They are a true mother and father in the faith! Enjoy and be encouraged.*"

—Dr. Dan Hammer, Senior Apostolic Leader
Sonrise Christian Center, Everett, Washington

"It is an honor to write an endorsement for a woman of God like Jervae Brooks. Her stories contained in 'Sustained for the Journey' will inspire you to trust God no matter what kind of challenges you face. Her story reminds me of Psalm 18, 'In my distress I called to the Lord... He rescued me from my powerful enemy (verses six & seventeen).' Time and time again, Jervae faced impossible situations, and as a woman of prayer, time and time again, God did miracles. Whatever kind of distress you may find yourself in during your journey, you will be encouraged by this book."

—Pastor John Hammer, Senior Pastor
Sonrise Christian Center, Everett, Washington

"This story will bring you on a journey with Jervae through some of the deepest valleys of her life. It is engaging from start to finish and gives a beautiful window into the pain, the struggles, and difficulties of each event, yet always gently pointing to the source of her strength; a loving heavenly Father. She is raw, transparent, and truthful. People who are going through horrible things don't want sugar coating; they want truth and honesty. Jervae has given them that."

—Martha Stanley, friend and collaborator
Publications Designer, Creative Services Dept.,
Aglow International
Tarpon Springs, Florida

"*Winston Churchill famously said, 'If you're going through hell, don't stop.' Jervae's story tells of God's faithfulness to never leave nor forsake you. Rather than walking through hell, join Jervae and her husband's journey through the valley of the shadow of death and out the other side, all the while retaining faith for the impossible and seeing God's faithfulness in all things big and small. As you join Jervae's story, you cannot help but be strengthened in your faith and resolve that God is good all the time.*"

—Kent R. DaVault, English professor and author

Table of Contents

Prologue: Finding Hope for Life's Journey

We all have our own individual story of beginnings, especially those times when we first head out from the relative safety and confines of our youth with family, school, and childhood events. I come from a strong Norwegian heritage, with ancestors on both my mom and dad's sides of the family having emigrated from Norway. They were all people of strength and character, hardworking, determined to find and follow their own path.

It seems to me that the path of life is like a journey—a series of journeys, actually. We often think of a journey as a holiday to some far-off destination, long-anticipated and planned down to the smallest detail. Those journeys are filled with excitement, and happy memories are recorded in photo albums and stories to recount at family gatherings held over the years.

Other journeys are those that take place when we move from one town to another, re-organizing our lives in a new environment. Those journeys are anticipated and planned for sure but are certainly not holidays.

The journeys I was most familiar with in my childhood years were those that took our family from living in one home and town to another.

During my younger years, my family moved quite often due to my dad's work in the newspaper business. It was in the days of home newspaper delivery, and he was in charge of the paperboy programs in one region of the state or another. It was always great fun when he would open the trunk of his company car and show my sister and me all the prizes he kept there for his awards to the paperboys he oversaw in the various towns. Sometimes we were allowed to choose one of those little treasures for ourselves. They were mostly boy things, like baseballs or pocket knives, because not many girls had paper routes in those days.

Most of our family's moves were in Minnesota, but for one year during my grade school days, we lived in Oklahoma. The move back to Minnesota was certainly a journey to remember. It was 1959, and all our household possessions were packed onto my uncle's hay wagon that he had pulled from central Minnesota to Oklahoma City for the move back north. What a sight we must have been!

My husband and I have always been pretty adventurous, enjoying camping trips with our three daughters when they were young and driving cross-country to visit relatives. Those journeys gave us many great memories. And after the kids were grown, we enjoyed some great trips on our motorcycle, traveling and tent camping all over the Western United States.

But there are other journeys during our lives that cannot be anticipated or planned. Those are the times when life takes a turn that leads us down a path so challenging it takes every ounce of strength and courage we can muster to navigate our way through. I have experienced my share of those journeys also; some would say more than my share.

While my story might be called an autobiography, or a memoir, I am writing to fulfill a deep desire in my heart to contemplate all the mountains and valleys of my life. It is one of the ways I wish to honor the God who carried me, led me, and sometimes dragged me over and through them!

I am also writing for my family and all those who are dear to me, helping them know the God I serve more deeply and hopefully carrying on our legacy of a loving Jesus to our future generations.

Above all, I am writing for all of you who are battling life's circumstances. There may be events in your life that took place years ago, but the struggle is still very real today. Or there may be events that you are walking through right now, and you are weary, wondering how you can go on.

I pray that through my testimony of God's sustaining strength, love, and courage, you might discover—or re-discover—His strength on the inside of you. And I pray that God's gifts of strength and hope will sustain you, helping you to persevere through your own challenges and personal battles—all the journeys of your life—to God's perfect peace.

This is a story about redemption. It is also a story of the realities of spiritual warfare and victory when the power of God overtakes the darkness. It is a story of the most devastating loss any parent can face, and of serious illnesses and desperation in the face of hopeless situations—and the awesome power of God to heal.

It is a testimony of love and of faith to believe God's promises. It is about being sustained for the journey and seeing how God's glory overshadows it all.

In my first book, *A Battle for Destiny*, I shared my testimony of faith and perseverance in God's grace and healing power. There are chapters yet to be chronicled—that took place before that journey in 2008—and some dramatic stories to tell in these years since then. That is what you will find on the following pages.

Three times my husband, Dwight, has experienced a life-threatening health crisis. The first happened in 1988. Twenty years later, in 2008, was the second, and the third crisis of health was in 2018 when the battle over cancer entered our journey. During each of those three frightening events, I had doctors tell me that my husband's situation was hopeless, that he could not survive. But God had other plans.

In 1992 another kind of struggle began; the struggle of devastating grief after the loss of a child.

After our daughter died, I read all the books I could find on grief, and especially those written by parents who had lost a child. I felt if they had lived through the pain of that loss, maybe, just maybe, I could too. Well, as you can see, I did live through it, and as the fullness of healing came into my heart and life, I often thought about writing about my experience through that journey.

Many times, I wondered if the world needed another book about what happens to a family when a child dies. There were already so many. But vivid memories fueled my thoughts.

I remembered the woman I met in Norway while traveling for Aglow, whose baby had died after birth while still in the hospital. All she knew for sure what that her baby was lying inside a box in the cold ground of the cemetery by the church. She showed me a large, framed photograph of her baby, clearly not alive, dressed in a pastel newborn baby dress. We both wept as I explained that her baby was not cold and alone in that coffin. Jesus had been there to carry the spirit of her sweet daughter to heaven with Him, and after we prayed the prayer of salvation together, this dear mother was certain that she would see her child again.

And I remembered speaking at an Aglow conference in Argentina where I had been asked to include the testimony of losing a child in my message. After the session, a dear woman came to me, shaken and weeping. She had lost her daughter eleven years before and had never once heard that her broken heart could be healed and that she could find joy again. We wept together as she asked Jesus to open the door of her heart for His precious peace to come in. Yes, Jesus can heal our broken hearts. He can also come to gently remove even the hardened scars of a heart broken long ago.

I spoke with a woman during a brief conversation while again traveling for Aglow in Australia, and somehow the subject of losing a child came up. She had her three sons with her, and I asked how they had coped with losing their brother. She responded, "Oh, we've never talked about it. We don't talk about him; he's just gone." My heart wept for her, and I shared just a little in the few moments we had together about how important it is to talk about these things in a family so that real healing can come. I've thought of that family since then and pray that short conversation helped lead them to a path back to wholeness.

The story you are about to read is true and unembellished. It all happened to me and my husband. We give thanks and praise to our Lord and Savior Jesus Christ for everything that He has done.

Every journey has a point of embarkation, a launching place, a beginning. A time when anticipation may be high, but we have no clear vision of all that is to come. Dwight and I were married in 1970 and were very much committed to one another in our marriage. But in those early years, I was about to find out how little I really knew about my husband. We had shared so much with each other, but we had not talked about what God meant to us. That was about to change dramatically as we began our journey through life together. God, in His love and power to redeem us from our frailties and mistakes, was about to show Himself mighty.

Thoughts to ponder

- Are there situations in your life—past or current—that you feel are hopeless?
- Do you believe God's power and love can reach into every situation in your life and bring healing and restoration?

Note: I believe everything that happens to us is for a reason. God uses every high and every low to teach us and grow us up to be the people He intended us to be from the beginning. And I also know that, very often, we learn lessons in our own lives through hearing the experiences of others.

I never wanted to write a book that would just tell a long sad story of things that happened in our life's journey. I wanted to tell a true story that could be used to bring meaning and hope to the difficult times in other people's lives. And to be honest, I wanted to give purpose to the heartaches and losses I had experienced in my own life.

At the end of each chapter, there are a few questions or statements I call "thoughts to ponder" that I hope will give you food for thought as you seek to find God's path for you in the midst of your own circumstances.

Chapter i
California Days ~ 1968

It was the summer of 1968, and I had moved west to live with my dear aunt Shirlee and uncle Ski and my wonderful "California cousins," Nancy and John. I had been going to college in Minnesota the year before, but I really could not afford the tuition, and my grades did not give me any help either. So, when my aunt invited me to come and live with them in Southern California, as another cousin had done some years before, I thought, *Why not?*

It was quite an adventure for this small-town Minnesota girl to head off to California, driving her huge 1956 Chrysler Imperial! It was my first car, and my dad had bought it for me from a little old lady near the central Minnesota town where we lived. It had been parked in her garage for years with the original plastic still on the back seat! "A good sturdy car to keep you safe," he had told me.

Another girl my age decided to make the trip with me—she was a "friend of a friend," and we met for the first time just the day before our cross-country trip began. She was also going to visit an aunt and uncle in California, and it was quite an exciting and first-time adventure for us both. Our second night on the road took us all the way to Las Vegas. Neither of us had ever seen such sights!

We found our motel in Las Vegas, where we had made reservations, and I called my parents to tell them we were doing okay. I remember telling them how hot it was, even though it was past dark! We went to a stage show and saw *Diana Ross and the Supremes*, feeling thrilled at the experience. After the show, we went to a nearby restaurant for pancakes, at about 2:00 a.m. We were not in small-town Minnesota anymore!

That sturdy car made the trip fine, and we arrived safe and sound in Southern California. I had never been there before and felt excited to live in such an amazing place. The Pacific Ocean! Mountains! Watching *The Tonight Show with Johnny Carson* and realizing it was happening just miles from where I was living! Wow.

Every experience in those days was new and exciting. I started applying for jobs and tapped into every ounce of courage as I headed out each day to find my way around the city. No GPS in those days! My aunt Shirlee would give me directions on how to get to the location of my interview, and I always found my way but often would somehow discover "new ways" to drive home again. One day, I found myself on a special through-road that ran diagonally across the greater Long Beach area as a quick way to get from one corner of the city to the other. Very few on or off-ramps, which in themselves were a new experience for me! My hometown in Minnesota didn't even have a stoplight! (And still doesn't to this day!) When I finally found my way back home and related to my aunt all the interesting things I saw along the way, she laughed, saying I had seen every corner of the city that afternoon!

It was like a dream come true living with my dear cousins, John and Nancy. Growing up, we only had short weeks in the summer together when their family came to Minnesota on vacation. Now we could deepen our relationship and enjoyed being together. To this day, we are the best of friends.

It was 1968, and the Vietnam War was raging. Of course, I heard the news every day, but the reality of Vietnam was far from my understanding or even my concerns, to be honest.

One experience I've thought of many times since those early days in California was going to a house party with my cousin John and his girlfriend in one of the trendy beach communities south of Los Angeles. I was having fun this evening with cool California college students and feeling on top of the world.

At one point, I was sitting out on the porch of this house visiting with a nice-looking young man with a short haircut and pressed shirt and trousers. He blended right in with the other people there at the party, and I thought he was a college student like the others. We made small talk for a few minutes, but he didn't have much to say. *Just shy*, I thought.

But it wasn't long before he stood up and walked away down the driveway. He didn't say goodbye or anything; he just left. I asked my cousin about him, and he told me the young man was in the Army and had just come back to the States on leave.

Although I did not realize it at the time, I had just met a representative of thousands of young adults in my generation. I had been given an up-close and personal glimpse of a young man who had been thrown into an experience that would forever change his life and, even then, had no words to explain or to understand it. In the months to come, I would meet many other young men like him, struggling to make sense of the confusing and dangerous life they had been drafted into. (Including my future husband—we'll get to that later.) How long would it take for any of them to find redemption in their own souls from things they had seen or experienced in the throes of a vicious and unpopular war and all the rage and emotions that came along with it?

As I have learned over the years what the Vietnam War was like and how it affected—and still is affecting—the lives of thousands of Americans, I have remembered that young man. Very likely, he had been on patrol in the jungles of Vietnam just a day or two before, fearing for his life, and here he was in a house party with a bunch of California college kids who had no real understanding of that war we were engaged in. Many of them would have even been quick to join a protest, given the chance. The late '60s in Southern Cal was quite the hotbed of emotion! It would be some years before I really developed a true understanding myself of all the things our country and that generation went through in those years.

Another more recent memory floods my mind of a young soldier I briefly met a few years ago while traveling for Aglow. I was waiting at the Frankfurt Airport for my flight back to the US and sat next to a twenty-something ruddy-faced young man. He was dressed in military fatigues and carrying a duffle bag. I thanked him for his service and asked where he was coming from. He quietly explained he had just left Afghanistan and was going home to Wisconsin for his father's funeral. My heart ached for him.

Our flight was called, and as I walked behind this young man down the passageway to our plane, I noticed sunburn on the back of his neck. Sunburn, not from working in the cornfields of Wisconsin on his father's farm, but from the dangerous and dusty hills of Afghanistan. Another memory hidden away in my heart. I've often thought of that young man, praying he came home safely, life and limb.

So in 1968, I became a "California girl." I found a job, began taking some night courses at the local college, and thoroughly enjoyed living with my aunt, and uncle, and cousins. Nothing wildly exciting, but I found everything interesting and new.

I finally was hired at a small business office near Compton, California. That part of Los Angeles was quite a center of turmoil in the late '60s. It had grown to be mainly an African American community with high unemployment and poverty. Not a good combination, but I always felt safe and did not experience any problems. I learned to love twenty-five-cent homemade Mexican bean burritos from the family-owned restaurant next to the office (the only restaurant lunch I could afford to splurge on once in a while) and even developed a taste for Mexican hot sauce! As silly as it sounds, that was a brand new taste for me! My world was expanding.

But my Minnesota roots were deep, and when I went home for Christmas that year, I felt the "pull" to move back to the more familiar lifestyle and my old group of friends. I think I was feeling a bit overwhelmed with life in general, and Minnesota felt a little "safer" in the long run. So I decided I would go back to California, quit my job, and return to Minnesota. But, as it turned out, my plans were short-lived.

While I was away for Christmas, my cousin Nancy met a handsome sailor named Tony. Tony had come to my aunt and uncle's home to visit Nancy with a young man I'll call Jimmy, a shipmate who was the son of friends of the family. My aunt and uncle were retired Navy people and knew the sailors enjoyed getting off the ship any time they could. They loved having the young men come to spend time at their house for an afternoon or evening, just visiting or watching TV and enjoying a home-cooked meal. Jimmy often brought friends, and that is how Tony had come during the Christmas break while I was away—and how another young sailor named Dwight happened to come with Jimmy for a visit just a few days after I had come back from Christmas in Minnesota. The four of us drove to a nearby ice cream shop for a Coke and enjoyed small talk for an hour or so. They weren't in uniform, and I really didn't have much frame of reference to what Navy life was like for them. They were just nice guys, and when they drove Nancy and me home again, before they left Dwight asked me if I'd like to go on a date with him the following Saturday night. I said, "Sure," and he left.

During the week, Dwight called me one night just to chat. We talked for a bit, and then he started saying goodbye. He hadn't said anything about our upcoming date, so I asked him what time he would pick me up. I had no way of knowing how important that innocent question was! He told me several years later—after we were already married—that if I hadn't said anything about the date, he was not going to show up. He had a secret he knew he would have to tell me, and he felt sure it would bring an end to our relationship before it had even begun.

Saturday night came. Dwight picked me up in his '57 Ford, and off we went to the "Cinnamon Cinder" in Long Beach for some music and dancing. He was clean-cut and quiet, not much for dancing, but we talked and laughed and enjoyed our evening together.

When he brought me home, and we pulled up in front of my aunt's home, he suddenly became very quiet. He sat looking straight ahead with both hands gripping the steering wheel, and I could tell he was trying to get up the nerve to tell me something. Finally, after several minutes of sitting in silence, he blurted out, "I'm married, and I have two kids."

What an outburst of true confession! I was nineteen years old, and here was this sailor telling me shocking news on our first date. I guess he was pretty sure it would also be our last date, but he knew he had to tell me. I have thought of that many times since and so admire the courage and character it took for him to be open and honest at that moment. When I didn't jump out of the car in horror and slam the door, I guess he thought maybe he would dare to call me again.

What allowed me to react in such a quiet way at that moment? I didn't really know this guy yet and had no commitment of any kind to him. But I was impressed by the way he openly answered the questions I asked him that night about his marriage and the children. There was something about this young man that intrigued me. I liked him and felt there was a lot more to know about him. The understatement of the year for sure! But he was open to share his story with me and later said he was impressed that what I learned about him didn't scare me away.

Dwight had married when he was just out of high school. He and his first wife were both very young and had married for the wrong reasons. When he joined the Navy, just before he would have been drafted into the Army, they moved to San Diego, where Dwight was stationed on a Navy ship. Life was hard and bleak, and when their first daughter, Terry, was born in 1966, things became even more difficult.

When their second daughter, Toni, was born just twelve and a half months later, their lives and their marriage began to unravel. Dwight's duties on ship were demanding, especially with it being wartime. In the late 1960s, the Vietnam War was raging and taking its toll on our nation as well as all the young men and their families who were serving in the military.

By 1968, Dwight had learned his wife was severely neglecting both little girls as well as physically and emotionally abusing them. Toni was just an infant and was being left alone in the house by her mother while Dwight was away on the ship. It all became overwhelming, and then the day came that his wife left him. Neither he nor the children ever saw her again.

Unable to get a hardship discharge, being wartime, Dwight arranged for Terry and Toni to live with a relative until his tour in the Navy was completed. It was just then—as he was figuring out where his sweet daughters could live while he completed his military service and before he was shipped out for Southeast Asia—that he and I met.

We started dating and saw each other nearly every weekend unless he had duty on the ship. His ship was in dry-dock for repairs in Long Beach, so he was able to come and see me often and spend time with the family. My aunt and uncle loved him, and as time went on, my grandmother actually told me I was going to marry him someday. She and Grandpa wintered with us in California, so Dwight got to know them too. I said, "Oh, Grandma, I don't think so. He's a nice guy but really isn't my type." Famous last words!

After several months I felt we were getting too serious, so I stopped accepting every single date—he would ask me out for the next weekend each time he brought me home. I guess he didn't want any of those other sailors who might have also visited our house with Jimmy to get any ideas. But one Saturday night that spring, I wouldn't accept his next date when he brought me home. This time I held to my decision and didn't change my mind.

The next morning after I came home from church, my cousin, my aunt, and I were in the kitchen fixing lunch. Suddenly there was a knock on the back door, and there stood Dwight with his two-year-old daughter, Terry. (By that time, one-year-old Toni had already been taken to live with a relative. Soon after this, Terry also went there to live until Dwight was discharged from the Navy.) I had not met Terry before and was so surprised to see them. She was such a pretty little thing, with long blonde hair, nicely brushed and hanging way down her back, wearing a sweet little red and yellow dress and shiny black shoes. Dwight said he had just "happened" to be driving by and wondered if I would like to go to the park with them. My aunt and cousin encouraged me to go, so off we went to a nearby park to watch Terry play at the playground.

After a short time, we left the park, and Dwight asked if I wanted to take a little drive. As he drove, he suggested that we stop in at his brother's house. He and his brother were in the Navy together in the "brother program," and he and his wife lived in a small apartment near the Navy base. I said no, it was lunchtime, and we couldn't just drop in. But he said it would be fine. When we got there, she had the table set for four (five with Terry) with lunch waiting for us!

They had it all planned. I stopped refusing Dwight's invitations for the next date, and before long, we were talking about getting married. Now he teases me that I married him for his kids!

One Saturday morning, he brought me to a jewelry store in Long Beach, and we bought a diamond ring, making our engagement official. Before he shipped out for his last tour of duty, he helped me move up to the Seattle area, where we planned to live after we were married. His parents and other siblings lived in a suburb north of Seattle, and by now, his brother and his wife that I had met in Long Beach were discharged from the Navy and living there too. So I wasn't alone but surely felt lonely when Dwight left for overseas again.

I found a job in Seattle, wrote letters to Dwight every day, numbering them because he would receive bunches at a time, and then he could at least read them in order and waited for his return from Vietnam.

I did what I could to stay connected to Terry and Toni, my soon-to-be daughters, with phone calls and letters to the relatives with whom they were living in Concord, California. I could not afford to see them often but once was able to fly down from Seattle to spend the weekend with them. Terry was only three and Toni two, and they were being lovingly spoiled by the dear family they lived with for that year and a half or so. We had a long way to go, but we were becoming a family.

Dwight and I were married on April 11, 1970, just two weeks after he returned from his final tour of duty overseas and upon his return to the States. My dear mom had always dreamed of planning a big wedding for me and expected me to move home for a year to prepare for the grand event. It was not an easy phone call when I had to explain that we wanted to just have a simple wedding in Seattle so we could finally unite our little family and start our lives together. After a number of phone calls back and forth, she and my dad understood, although my dad had a grocery store to run and could not make plans to be away so quickly. In the end, my mom flew out to be with us at our wedding, held in my cousin's home in Renton, to watch us be married in front of a judge. Dwight's mom made the cake, his brother and wife were our witnesses, and we decorated with vases of flowers bought at the local country market. Big beautiful weddings are wonderful, but to date, our simple one has lasted over fifty years.

Two months after our wedding, we traveled to Minnesota for a wedding reception my mom and dad had planned for us. We stood with the pastor at the altar in our Lutheran church in front of all my family, dressed in our wedding clothes, and again recited our wedding vows. So now we were "really" married in the church and in front of my loving dad. The memory of Dad sitting in the church pew and watching me intently is sweet and still touches my heart.

Wedding photo: April 1970

Jervae and Terry, age three and a half,
Toni, age two and a half, June 1970

Thoughts to ponder

- Have your "fairytale plans" ended up quite differently than you expected? How have you handled this in your life?
- As you look at the journey through your early years, even if you were not following the Lord at the time, in what ways can you see His hand upon you directing your way?

CHAPTER 2:

Many New Beginnings ~ 1970

In early 1970, Boeing, Seattle's largest employer at the time, was forced to cut its workforce by over half due to changes in airline programs and order cancellations. Recession set in, and by April 1971, a billboard was erected near Sea-Tac International Airport that read, "Will the last person leaving Seattle—turn out the lights." Dwight was hired on at US Plywood at the job he had before he enlisted in the Navy, working on the "green line," feeding wet veneer for making plywood into the dryer. A good muscle builder for sure, but not a long-term job.

We had always planned to bring our daughters up from California to Seattle to begin living as a family, but instead, we decided to become part of the mass exodus from Seattle and move to where they had been living, in Concord, California.

We loaded up the car with all our possessions—furnished apartments allowed us to travel light in those days—and joined our daughters in California. Dear "Nana," the grandmother of my future sister-in-law, with whom they had lived for the past two years and who had lovingly and completely taken them into her heart, came to our apartment to care for them while I worked to help in their transition. We are eternally grateful to dear Nana and her large Italian family, who nurtured and loved Terry and Toni during those early years.

We found an apartment in Concord and suddenly were a family of four. I took to motherhood quickly and loved being a mommy to our instant family of two little girls, three and four years old by then. Dwight and I were both working, and Nana came to our apartment to care for the girls during the day. Married life had begun!

Our first Christmas, 1970

Two years later, in 1972, my dad invited us to come to Minnesota to help him manage his grocery store in my hometown of Browerville, with plans to eventually buy the store from him when he was ready to retire. We talked long and hard about his offer, knowing it would be a very different lifestyle, especially for Dwight. He knew nothing about the grocery business—or about living in a small mid-Western town! But we decided it would be a good move for our family, so off we went to Minnesota, our 1967

Buick Wildcat pulling a ten-foot trailer. The load was too much for our car, so we couldn't use the air conditioner on the long trek from California. It was a dusty, sweaty family who finally reached Browerville that hot summer day.

Living in a small town is unique, and I loved it. My experiences with small towns have led me to believe that each little town, some parts of the world would call them villages, have their own personality. I don't know why that is, but it surely has something to do with the types of individuals living in that town that make up the whole. If you drive five to seven miles in any direction out of our central Minnesota town of Browerville, population 750, you will find another town about the same size. Some a little smaller, some larger. If you live in that type of area, you'll know what I mean. It has something to do with it being roughly a days' ride by horseback between towns, from when the towns first came into existence. Really very practical.

Browerville was a community surrounded by farms and made up of strong, hardworking families. Most were German or Polish, with a few Scandinavians as well who had settled in the area generations ago. The large Catholic church was attended by the majority of the people, with others, mostly the Scandinavians, going to the smaller Lutheran church. My family was of the latter group.

All the while I was growing up, I didn't actually know anyone who went to an Assembly of God church or one of the Pentecostal denominations. Looking back, I now see that my religious understanding was very narrow. But I had a strong faith, was always involved in our church, and felt a real closeness to God.

We had a good life in Browerville, and Dwight began learning the grocery business, soon becoming "the meat man." He adapted quickly to small-town life and soon was well known throughout the community. In those days, we delivered groceries to those who requested that service, and Dwight was especially popular with the elderly women because he was always friendly, and they enjoyed their little visits with him when he brought in their groceries, setting the bags on their kitchen table. Often they insisted on giving him a homemade cookie or glass of lemonade before he left—sweet moments in their day, and in his too.

I also worked in the grocery store along with Dwight and my mom and dad. But I longed to have a baby, and in 1974, God blessed us with a third daughter, Tracy. It's a miracle he didn't miss the birth of our daughter because he had planned to be out fishing very early that holiday morning. It was July 4, and she wasn't actually due for a couple of weeks, so he had planned to skip the family 4th of July barbecue and go fishing instead. Thankfully for me, Tracy let us know well before he left for the lake that we would be having other plans that day!

Terry and Toni were excited to have a baby sister to help care for and play with. Terry was the "little mama," and our photo albums from back then show many pictures of Terry with baby sister Tracy happily riding on her hip. My life was full, with three sweet daughters, family, and friends.

There were, however, difficult times in those years too, when life just seemed too hard, and the "go-to" solution for us was turning to alcohol. Both Dwight and I had developed a strong drinking habit over the past few years, and most weekends, we found some reason to party and always ended up drinking way too much.

Dwight was well-liked by our friends and respected as a fair, friendly, and honest businessman in town. But he also had gained the reputation of a hard-drinking guy whose main interests were out in the woods or on a lake somewhere. Dwight and my dad were well known at the town's bar/liquor store and Vets Club. A fun time was had by all when Kenny and Dwight were around.

Dwight was finding it a struggle to get his bearings in life and in working with my dad. Deep frustrations began to surface, and at one point, he had even considered re-enlisting in the Navy, but that did not seem to be the answer. One night when he was feeling particularly frustrated and fueled by too much whiskey, Dwight and I were arguing about something now long-forgotten but at the time had us both very upset. In the heat of the moment, Dwight said to me, "Well, maybe we should just get a divorce!" I didn't get angry very often, but this instantly roused me to anger. He had divorced once before, and I was not about to have our marriage end that way! I yelled back at him, "Don't you *ever* say that word to me again! You're stuck with me, and I'm stuck with you, and we'll just need to figure this out!"

He knew I was really mad, and I think I shocked him a bit. He never again threatened divorce. At this writing, we've been married for more than fifty years! Praise God! Many times it has not been easy, but each time we have "figured it out!"

Even though we had our "issues," as they say today, I felt we had a pretty good marriage. We loved each other and were committed to each other and to our family. But one major point of contention was in Dwight refusing to come to church with me and the girls. He came with us on Easter and Christmas, but that was all. He knew it was important to me and that, even when I was living on my own, before we were married, I went to the local Lutheran church wherever I was living at the time on most Sundays. We talked a lot about many things, but he would never open up and tell me why he refused so strongly to come to church. I had no idea the secrets about himself that he was hiding from me.

Our lives revolved around long hours in the grocery store, raising our three young daughters, and hearty partying on the weekends. Actually, our lives were not so different from many of our friends' lives. But a significant hidden difference was that my husband, deep in his heart, was an angry young man full of festering hurts and resentments that he had never faced. While we did have mostly good times together, and I knew he loved me and our daughters, that frustration and anger were always simmering just below the surface. But God had a plan for Dwight's life—and mine as well! A series of events were about to unfold that would change our life's path dramatically.

It was May of 1975, and a small group of friends from our (my) Lutheran church in Browerville had gathered for an evening of food and fellowship. We had decided to form what we called a "Young Couples Club," with a plan to meet once a month for a home meeting to have conversations around some meaningful topic. In that small town of 750 people, we already knew each other well, but we felt a drawing to have this focused time to grow deeper in our faith.

I was happy when Dwight agreed to go with me to the first meeting, even though this was a "church event." After all, the group was made up of friends in town that we both knew, so he felt safe. Neither of us knew that innocent-sounding evening was actually a "set up" designed by God to put us on a path that would begin to bring about His purposes. God had His eye on both of us, and things were about to change!

This meeting of our Young Couples Club was held at the home of a couple who had a lovely piece of land a few miles out of town. They had moved north from the metropolitan area of Minneapolis/St. Paul, a few years before with a dream of raising their family in the country and living off the land. Easier said than done, they soon learned, but they had a comfortable little home, beautiful acreage around a pretty pond, and a peaceful "corner of the world" to pursue their dreams.

That evening, our planned activity was to take a walk through their woods, full of new growth on the trees and lovely spring flowers. We also had invited our pastor to come that evening and talk with us about some unusual and interesting things we had begun to hear about. The charismatic movement had begun in the early 1970s, and just a few weeks before this eventful evening, one of the couples had been invited to attend a Lutheran charismatic conference. The word "charismatic" was completely new to all of us. But rather than thinking it was too different or weird, a wonderful curiosity began to grow. Our friends had come home from that conference with stories of having seen and heard of amazing things that were happening in the lives of people who knew Jesus in a different way than we had ever even heard about before. Our pastor had professed to be "Spirit-filled," whatever that was, and we were eager to have him sit with us and explain these wonders.

Most of us had been going to church our whole lives and had gone through all the traditional steps of our Lutheran faith. We had been baptized as infants, which we were taught represented our salvation in Jesus, and we had gone through confirmation, which were the weekly classes at church designed to teach us about our faith, culminating in becoming confirmed as "adult" members of the church. This wonderful moment was also meant to bring the infilling of the Holy Spirit into our young lives. We were as true as we knew to be to the tenets of our Lutheran faith, but at least for me, no lasting change had happened in my life. I am sorry to admit that confirmation to me meant that I could start wearing nylon stockings and high-heeled shoes to church on Sunday mornings!

For most of us, our faith was superficial compared to the things our friends had seen and heard about at that charismatic conference. This was the mid-1970s, the Jesus People Movement had begun, and we suddenly began to learn about a relationship with Jesus that we had never before known existed. Every time I met with my friends for coffee, with our young children playing at our feet, questions filled our conversations. Where we had always talked about our flower or vegetable gardens, potty training, and the latest recipes, we were now talking about God! A "holy curiosity" began to grow in our hearts. An amazing heavenly plan was about to burst forth. All questions, no answers, and wondering if the things we had heard about were real.

But God was about to use it all for His glory and to set our lives in a brand new direction. Looking back, we see the loving, purposeful hand of God steadily directing us toward Himself.

Our first Young Couples Club evening was progressing well. We had enjoyed our walk through the woods, had rid ourselves of the pesky ticks we all had carried back to the house—a natural task after a springtime walk in the Minnesota woods—and were settled in our friend's living room with our plates of dessert and coffee. We began our conversation with the pastor, asking him our questions as we all tried to gain some simple, beginning understanding of the wonders of God we had been hearing about. Very elementary questions like, what is the Holy Spirit? What is speaking in tongues? What does it mean to be filled with the Holy Spirit? Our dear pastor was trying to answer our questions but struggling, I believe, with the intensity with which we all wanted to know! We were seeking more than the answers provided in the Lutheran catechism, and the atmosphere in the room held an almost painful longing to really know more of God than we ever had known before.

Suddenly my husband—who everyone in the room knew to be an adamant non-church attender, prone to be hot-tempered and more interested in fishing, hunting, and partying than anything to do with God or church, spoke up from his place on the sofa. He had been sitting quietly listening to many in the group asking our pastor these questions, but no real answers were coming forth. As I later learned, he was becoming so frustrated that he finally could stay silent no longer.

All eyes turned to look with surprise at my husband when he said, "I can answer some of those questions." All of us, including me, looked at him in disbelief. What could he possibly know concerning the questions about the Holy Spirit that we were discussing that evening? He didn't attend church, never read the Bible, and to my knowledge, never had! That admission from my husband was met by a stunned silence and opened the door to something we could not have imagined at that moment. Our questions had been simple ones but profound in our lack of understanding.

Dwight began to speak, giving simple but direct answers to the questions we had expressed. He even shared a few scripture references. He knew where these stories were in the Bible! He spoke as someone who really understood these mysteries and knew them to be true. He spoke as someone who knew God in the way the rest of us were seeking. This was amazing, surprising, and more than a little scary. This was Dwight, and we all knew him—or thought we did! How could he possibly know about things like this?

With all of us stunned into shocked silence and unable to think of any more questions, the evening came to an end. We all packed up our children and left for home.

Our friends lived several miles out of town. It was dark as we drove home, and I can remember looking out my passenger window of the car seeing the Big Dipper. I enjoyed finding the Big Dipper in the northern sky at night. Always there, always the same. I saw it again that night. But now, nothing was the same, and as I would soon learn, our lives would never be the same again. It has been well over forty years, and even now, when I see the Big Dipper, I remember that night. Now I remember and thank God for what He did for us.

Dwight and I didn't talk much as we drove home. I really didn't know what to say to him. We had been married for five years, had three daughters, and for the most part, a good marriage. But at that moment, I felt as though I did not even know him anymore.

I've thought of this so many times and wondered why I had never asked him if he was a Christian. I didn't even realize it at the time, but I was pretty much a "Sunday morning Christian" myself, and now I know that my own relationship with God had been shallow. But God is a loving and jealous God, and He wanted all of us for Himself. A new life was about to begin.

We got home and put the girls to bed. We got into bed ourselves with a strange silence between us. Moments after lying down, Dwight got up and, without a word, went downstairs. I listened for the refrigerator door to open but heard nothing. I even listened for the car door to open and wondered if he was leaving! It had been such a strange evening already, and I didn't know what to expect.

Since his time in the Navy and serving in Vietnam, he had struggled in ways too deep for me to understand or to reach. He couldn't even handle his own emotions at times, and more than once, he had just taken off to sort out his feelings without my knowing when he might be coming home again. He never stayed away long and sometimes came back pretty drunk after trying to "drown" his troubles. Of course, that solved nothing.

After some minutes and hearing no sounds, I went downstairs to look for him. I found him sitting on the bare, wooden basement stairway. It was a chilly night in May, and he was sitting there in just his night clothes. He was crying. I had never seen him cry before. I slowly went down the stairs to sit on the step behind him until he could tell me what was happening.

Tears flowed from us both as he told me that when he lay down in bed, he immediately felt the finger of God poking him in the chest. God spoke to his heart, saying, "Who do you think you are! You are talking about Me like you know Me! But you are not living for Me! Who do you think you are!"

Dwight knew the time had come, and he had to get right with God! He had run from Him long enough. Hurts and disappointments had caused him to build a strong protective wall around his heart. His years serving in the US Navy and all the things he had experienced during the Vietnam War and in his first marriage had scarred his heart and his conscience in ways that left him hardened and afraid to trust God. He knew it wasn't right, but too many unhappy situations had taken over his life.

So he found that secluded spot on the cold basement stairway and asked God to forgive him. Immediately he "felt" a warm blanket come down around his shoulders, and instantly, he knew he was surrounded by his loving and forgiving heavenly Father. He began to weep hot tears of both repentance and thankfulness to God, who immediately welcomed him back as a much-loved son. Instantly, in the amazing way that only God can touch our inner being, Dwight felt accepted by God and bathed in His love.

Then Dwight asked God to restore his prayer language. I learned later that it had been years since he had used it, and he wasn't even sure if it was real at that time. Immediately he began to speak in an unknown language as he praised God with his spirit.

What? My own husband spoke in tongues? I was completely amazed. Dwight asked me to go back upstairs, and he would explain everything. When he came back to the bedroom, as we lay next to one another in bed, Dwight told me what had been happening on the inside of him that night. Then he asked me if he could pray for me. We had never prayed together before. He also asked me if he could pray for the Holy Spirit to fill me just as he had been filled a few minutes before.

We laid there side by side as he prayed for me to be surrounded by God's love, to be filled with the Holy Spirit, to receive my own prayer language that I could use to worship God in a brand new way. This man had changed before my very eyes.

After those minutes of that first prayer together with my husband, I, too, was changed. I still had lots of questions, my prayer language did not begin right away, but my questions were no longer gripping me. I was filled with peace, knowing God was the Lord of my life. He would teach me, and I would learn His ways. I was filled with the Holy Spirit and with the peace of God.

Finally, Dwight was able to tell me about all the secrets he had hidden deep inside. The walls around his heart came down. By the time we met, he had grown far away from any relationship with Jesus. Hurts, disappointments, and things he had seen and experienced as a sailor in the Navy all had led him away from God. So far away that he had never even hinted to me that such things were part of his younger life.

He had been running away from God, unable to face the hurts and disappointments of life. In all our five years of marriage, Dwight had never told me about the relationship he had with the Lord when he was a boy. He had never told me about the Holy Spirit-filled church he and his family had been part of, the miracles he had seen, the power of the Holy Spirit he knew was real. He had never told me he knew Jesus as his personal Lord and Savior and, even as a teenager, had been active in the church he and his family attended. More about that later.

The next day was Sunday. I was excited to tell my pastor what had happened to me. But when I told him what had happened to me the night before, he became upset with me, saying I had had it all along, through my infant baptism and confirmation when I was young. I told him that might have been true, but something had happened to me that I had never experienced before.

Now every part of our lives was being shaken and about to be turned upside down!

Thoughts to ponder

- Have you given yourself wholly over to the Lord? He is pursuing you! Can you feel it?
- God loves you so much and arranges things in our lives to lead us to Himself. What "holy coincidences" have happened in your life that have led you to a closer walk with Jesus?

CHAPTER 3:

Re-created and Redeemed ~ 1975

> Has the Lord redeemed you? Then speak out! Tell
> others He has saved you from your enemies.
>
> Psalm 107:2 (NLT)

I had met Jesus in a whole new way, and I was different. Dwight
and I were beginning a new life together. We had experienced an
encounter with the Holy Spirit and soon came to understand we
were part of the growing charismatic movement. It was all new
to us, and we had no words in those days to describe it. We just
knew Jesus had touched our hearts and was now more real to us
than we ever could have imagined.

If you are not familiar with the charismatic movement, or
some call it the Holy Spirit movement, I encourage you to read
about its beginnings. (Even Google has some good articles on
this subject.) The charismatic movement actually began in the
late 1950s among people in the Anglican church and continued
to grow in other Christian denominations in what began to be
called the Jesus movement in the '60s and '70s. Testimonies
throughout this time speak of dramatic encounters with God,
people receiving what is termed the baptism of the Holy Spirit
with the evidence of speaking in tongues. The gifts of the Spirit
spoken of in 1 Corinthians 12 are a vital part of the Spirit-filled

life of believers, given by the Holy Spirit to be used to minister to the needs of others.

Dwight had grown up in a Pentecostal-type church, so he had some background knowledge of what we were experiencing, even though it had never been so real to him as it became now. With my Lutheran background, I now know the catechism speaks of salvation, gifts of the Spirit, living our lives for Christ. But I had never before grasped the reality of Jesus like I had come to know Him.

Our lifestyle began to change right away, and many things that had been regular habits just fell away. As I said, both Dwight and I had been pretty heavy drinkers—not daily, but we were both quick to join the party and stay until the end. Something had changed inside of us to the point that neither of us had that desire any longer. This actually cost us some friends because they didn't know how to relate to the "new us." Our way of speaking also changed, and suddenly, we realized that it was no longer filled with off-color, coarse language like it had been for so long.

Back then, I had no idea what joys, adventures, and even heartaches lay ahead for us. I only knew that Jesus was more real than I had ever before imagined, and I wanted to follow Him with my whole heart. From that day to this, He has proved Himself faithful and loving to us through every situation our journey has taken us.

So that began an amazing season of discovery. We sought out places where we could learn about this new way to live. We were eager to get together with others who also had become "born again," and we began to meet new friends. The charismatic movement was in full swing, so we found many opportunities to learn together and deepen our faith.

On Saturday nights, we would drive forty-five miles to Alexandria, Minnesota, a larger town where a community of young believers who lived at the "Resurrection House" opened the large old home to anyone who wanted to come. These were evenings of singing lively praise choruses, worship to God, Bible teaching, and prayers spoken out that were anointed and deeply moving as if coming from the very heart of Jesus. Through all these types of ministry, we were learning how much He loved us and how to live the Spirit-filled life of a believer in Jesus Christ. It was exciting, fun, and 180° from what our Saturday nights had been like before!

Our definition of fun had certainly changed! Rather than drowning ourselves in alcohol on a Saturday night, we were now immersing ourselves in the pure "new wine," referring to what Jesus was offering by giving us a new understanding of who He is. And it was bringing us life.

We met some very interesting people in those days. We would attend our local Lutheran church on Sunday morning to "bloom where we were planted." And then, we would drive to attend a church service again in the afternoon or evening. In Alexandria, along with the Resurrection House, a new church had begun, and the weekly services were lively and exciting. The choruses we sang were filled with joy and meaning, helping us to grasp the concepts of God's love for us more fully. Every service held nuggets of new understanding.

I remember one Sunday afternoon; there were so many in attendance in that small church sanctuary that even in the altar area right around the pulpit, people were sitting on the floor eager to hear the Word of God being preached. The pastor was a young man with bright red hair, full of the Holy Spirit, who had a gift for teaching and bringing the scriptures to life. I remember his wife played the piano during the worship service, and the instrument almost "danced" across the floor with her lively playing. She had not had any musical training and didn't read music, but God had supernaturally given her the ability, and she and her husband were powerfully serving God together. What fun those lively Sunday afternoon church services were!

⌇

Those years in the mid-1970s were a time of growth and maturing in our walk with the Lord. A key area of that maturation process was in getting free from demonic strongholds that had found open doors in our lives through hurt, trauma, and losses. We were about to begin a crash course in spiritual freedom!

Those first weeks of our new lives in Christ were filled with joy and wonder. We were amazed at this new way of life and could hardly wait until the next time we could be in the midst of a prayer meeting or church service where the Holy Spirit was present and given full reign. Every time was exciting, and we were happy in ways we had never known before. There was a sense of contentment in knowing we were pursuing something good, something that would lead to fulfillment rather than destruction.

But there was someone who was definitely not happy. The enemy of our souls, who is Satan, despised what had happened to us. He had lost us to Jesus Christ, and he was not about to let us go easily. A struggle began that took us from happy oblivion right past basic training and straight into a battle for our lives.

When you read the Bible stories about Jesus in the Gospels of Matthew, Mark, Luke, and John, you see that Jesus' ministry included many references of delivering people from evil spirits.

He even sent out His twelve disciples for the first time with these instructions. "Jesus called his twelve disciples together and gave them authority to cast out evil spirits and to heal every kind of disease and illness" (Matthew 10:1, NLT).

Neither Dwight nor I had any experience with or knowledge of deliverance from evil spirits. Even though I knew the Bible spoke of these things, the little I knew about this type of ministry scared me. I didn't even want to hear stories from others about deliverance or any experience with spirits other than the Holy Spirit. I wanted to stay far away from anything that dealt with spiritual darkness. But we had become children of God, and Jesus was jealous for us. He wanted our whole lives.

The jealousy God has for us is often misunderstood. He is jealous for us because He loves us with a love too deep for our minds to fathom, and He knows what we need for our very best life. In Exodus 34:14, we read, "You must worship no other gods, for the Lord, whose very name is Jealous, is a God who is jealous about his relationship with you" (NLT).

He is jealous "about" His relationship with us, not "of" that relationship, or even "for" that relationship. He is jealous about it because of its value. He paid the price of death on the cross for a relationship with us and is lovingly and jealously guarding it—for our good and for His glory!

I want to share about some of the things God brought us through in our journey to spiritual freedom, not to be dramatic or to give attention to the enemy of our souls—who is Satan—but to testify about the power of God and the authority He gives to us when we accept His baptism in the Holy Spirit.

In sharing these things, I hope to bring light to some areas that you might be struggling with in your own life. In Luke

11:36, we read, "If you are filled with light, with no dark corners, then your whole life will be radiant, as though a floodlight were filling you with light" (NLT). Lord, we want to be filled with Your light! That was our prayer, and in that process, the darkness had to be dealt with.

Jesus was jealous for our whole being to be His. A season of "spiritual housecleaning" was about to begin and, just as important, a season of learning about the power and authority we carry through the Spirit of God inside of us.

Not long after our wonderful conversion that night in May of 1975, strange things began to happen in our home and to Dwight. We both were entering a time of training that we would never have imagined.

One night as we were going to sleep, Dwight suddenly began to thrash around in bed, screaming that "something" was trying to crawl into his body through his legs. Although neither of us had any instruction or training in how to deal with such things, we both immediately sensed that this was not a physical thing but a spiritual attack. Night after night for weeks, Dwight would experience similar attacks on his body, his mind, and his spirit. Somehow, our children stayed asleep during these middle-of-the-night battles, as Dwight fought the evil that was attacking him, and I battled in prayer over him.

During one such battle, we stood in the bathroom with Dwight retching over the commode and me standing behind him, laying my hands on him, praying. Suddenly he turned with fierce anger on his face, and in a voice that was not his own, he yelled at me to quit praying because it wasn't doing any good. I knew it was not my husband who was saying that to me because he didn't speak to me like that! And also, by now, I had learned my prayers were indeed powerful! So I began to pray all the more strongly and commanding the devil to leave. Soon the attack of the night ended with God's peace again settling upon us. Another skirmish won. But there were still bigger battles ahead before we could declare freedom.

We had become part of a small group of Spirit-filled believers in our area who met for prayer in one another's homes several times a month. The group was made up of four or five couples, most of whom were already leaders in the Christian community in our area. Dwight and I looked up to these people and considered them to be spiritually mature and able to help us in this intense time of spiritual battling that we found ourselves in. We shared with them the frightening experiences we were having nightly and asked them to pray for Dwight and cast off the spirits that were attacking him. We wanted it to be over and done with!

One night as we met, this particular time in our own home, they had come prepared to pray deliverance for Dwight, and both of us were expectant. We had a strong time of prayer, but none of us knew how to stand against the strength of this enemy that did not want to let him go. It was a time so intense that Dwight became convulsed by a force that was not of God, and blood vessels in his face ruptured as he fought against the forces trying to overtake him. Our dear friends were praying for us in good faith, but none of us knew how to fully access the power of God inside of us. The spiritual battle of that night was lost, and Dwight and I both knew we needed more help.

We learned of a family camp in northern Minnesota that had a strong focus on deliverance ministry. Remember, this was in the early days of the Jesus people movement. When I look back,

I see there were many people just like us who had turned our lives over to Jesus and were now living for Christ. And Satan was not happy about any of it. Centers like this sprang up, led by people who were mature in God and knew how to battle the darkness that had its hold on new believers. Thankfully, we found our way there, feeling hopeful.

I remember driving up to that camp in the late summer of 1976, with Dwight and I and our three daughters. We stayed in a cabin, and it was fun to be with other families, eating our meals together, listening to inspiring messages while our kids were having fun in the children's meetings. It was almost like a mini-vacation enjoying the camp's activities while we waited for our appointment for personal ministry time.

When our time came, we brought our daughters to enjoy play time with the other children, and we went to the room where the prayer team was waiting for us. We were a little nervous but also very expectant that God was going to intervene for us and bring freedom from the traumatic events we had been living through. There were four or five men and women, all mature Christians, who knew their authority in Christ. They gave instructions to both of us on how to stand in victory and encouraged us that we would find complete victory in Jesus. After talking for a while, they began to pray with power and authority in the name of Jesus, commanding the harassing evil spirits to come out and leave. The enemy of our souls, Satan, cannot stay when such commanding prayers are being said in the name of Jesus. It was an intense time, and we were both in awe of God's power as Dwight was delivered from a number of evil, oppressing spirits. We left the camp with our family greatly encouraged and refreshed, even though we knew there was still a bit more to be accomplished.

Some who are reading this might be wondering how Dwight could be filled with the Holy Spirit and harassed by evil spirits at the same time. I have pondered and studied this question too, and understanding this is very important for us all whenever we find ourselves in a spiritual battle.

Please understand I do not believe that a Christian can be demon-possessed. First Corinthians 7:23 states, "God paid a high price for you" (NLT). And if God has bought you, paid in full for you with His own life on the cross, then He owns you, and He will not let you go. But Satan is always looking for ways to harass us, oppress us, to try and cause us to stumble. He wants to fill our lives with pain or, at worst, turn us away from God altogether.

We all are made up of three parts—body, soul, and spirit. When we accept Jesus Christ as our Lord and Savior, we are "born again." Our spirit, which had been dead to Christ, comes alive. Christ now has authority over our spirit, and it cannot be possessed by anyone or anything but Christ. Praise God!

But our soul can be accessed by Satan or "oppressed." Satan will try to influence you to reject the Spirit of God. The Bible tells us we are to "Put on all of God's armor so that you will be able to stand firm against all strategies of the devil" (Ephesians 6:11, NLT).

The enemy of our souls uses strongholds to hinder or even prevent us from finding a deeper and more personal walk with Jesus. These might be walls we build around ourselves for self-protection against hurts, keeping others away who could encourage and love us. Or believing lies Satan tells us about ourselves and others, keeping us from living full lives and being all God intended us to be. It might be a traumatic experience caused through no fault of our own that opens the door for a demonic stronghold to enter. Satan will take every opportunity to destroy our relationship with Jesus Christ.

But dear one, know this! "For he has rescued us from the kingdom of darkness and transferred us into the Kingdom of his dear Son, who purchased our freedom and forgave our sins" (Colossians 1:13-14, NLT). Jesus bought your past. It does not belong to you anymore. While Jesus hung on the cross, your name was on His lips! Never be afraid to seek personal ministry to be set free from demonic oppression when Satan tries to mess with you!

Not long after our time at the deliverance camp, as autumn approached, we were praying with some dear friends who had been walking with us through this season and who had been a lifeline of hope to us both. That night, as we prayed, a "picture" in the spirit came to one of us. The picture was of a large tree with some big branches from that tree lying on the ground at its base. As the vision continued, these branches floated upwards to become part of the tree again. There had been many kinds of brokenness among Dwight's siblings. He was the oldest of seven, and we felt God was leading us to pray for the generations to come together in Dwight's family.

The next day, Dwight made phone calls to his siblings and shared about what he had been going through. They all had been raised in a Christian home, and their dear mother had taught them the power of prayer. They had stood together as a family through some very difficult times, and together, they had witnessed God's miraculous hand change their circumstances.

One of those times was when Dwight was about fourteen years old. His father had been severely affected emotionally by terrible things he had experienced in the US Army serving in Germany during World War II. One of the many symptoms he suffered was terrible ulcers covering the whole inside of his stomach. He was in the hospital scheduled for an extreme surgery that was used in those days, of removing his stomach and replacing it with a sheep's stomach. The surgery was risky, and recovery terrible. Dwight's mother needed a miracle to save her husband and the father of her seven children.

The night before the surgery, she packed Dwight, his five brothers, and baby sister into the car and drove to their home church. They went to the altar, and Dwight remembers lying on the steps at that altar, along with his mother and brothers and sister, weeping and praying all night long for their father's healing. The next morning, his mother returned to the hospital and insisted the doctors test her husband again before they did the surgery. To their utter surprise, they found his stomach had been completely healed. A brand new, healthy stomach had replaced the infected and ulcerated tissue. God had answered their prayers for a miracle.

Dwight said he came home from school the next day to find his father resting on the couch, still recovering from the anesthesia they had already begun to administer for the surgery when his mother made them stop to test his stomach again. Faith and power in prayer!

So, that day when he phoned his siblings, they talked about these things and remembered the God of their youth. The evils of the world had affected his brothers too, and that day three of them came back into a relationship with God. What a joyous day, and joyful too because we could see the victorious hand of God that had come forth in our lives.

Thoughts to ponder

- Honestly ask yourself if there are areas in your life that are not fully in God's control. Be open to someone praying with you to re-claim the true freedom you have in Christ Jesus.
- If you are born again, with the evidence of speaking in tongues, do you use your prayer language every day? It is your own personal and intimate way Jesus has given you to pray in direct connection to God. Praying in tongues is a key in spiritual warfare and will bring strength and peace to you.

CHAPTER 4:

Growing Deeper ~ 1976

Throughout the intense spiritual battles I experienced with Dwight, I somehow always had a deep faith that God would see us through to victory. I read Romans 10:17 (NLT), where it says, "So faith comes from hearing, that is, hearing the Good News about Christ." I read the scriptures and heard teachings about faith, and God gave me the strength to believe in faith in the middle of my circumstances. I admit it was scary at times, but I knew in my spirit that God's power was stronger than this enemy that had been harassing my husband and holding him captive.

Up to this time, the battle mainly involved Dwight. I was learning how to stand strong in prayer support of my husband and had felt the attacks on him, but I had not felt attacked myself. But Satan, the enemy of our soul, is relentless in trying to destroy any way he can. As this season of spiritual warfare was ending over Dwight's life in victory, a new and vicious attack came. This time it came upon me.

As women, we carry many things in our hearts, pondering and praying as we watch God working on things in our family, our circumstances, or in our own lives. Often those around us have no idea of all the things going on inside of us. (How many women who just read this are smiling to themselves right now?)

I had a struggle going on inside of me that few people around me knew about and of which no one knew the intensity.

I longed for another baby. We had always planned to have just one baby, feeling that a family of three children was just right for us. When Tracy was born, I felt content and that our three little girls perfectly completed our family. So, when Tracy was about a year old, we decided Dwight would take the permanent step of having a vasectomy, and we both were in agreement to do this.

But not long after this procedure was done, I was shocked to realize that I might be pregnant. I was nervous to tell Dwight because of the "final" decision we had already made and the painful medical procedure he had gone through! But when I told him, he was instantly excited about the possibility! I made an appointment with our family doctor and went in for the pregnancy test. It was positive! But the doctor also said there was something unusual in the examination, and he suggested that I come back in two weeks for a follow-up appointment, and at that time, he would give a second pregnancy test.

As I drove home from that first appointment, I was shocked at this sudden change that was coming to our lives, but couldn't help feeling excited that God was giving us another baby! We could not keep our joy a secret and began to tell family and friends that our family was growing. I began to "feel" pregnant and started planning like new mothers love to do.

After two weeks, I returned to the doctor for the follow-up test, feeling certain there was no question about my happy expectant condition. So when the doctor came into the room and told me the second test was negative, and the first one had actually been a "false positive," I was stunned. He told me I had never actually been pregnant, and he could not explain why the first test had been positive.

I was crushed, and worse yet, when I went home and told Dwight, he was as well. We didn't condemn ourselves for making the decision for Dwight to have the vasectomy, but now we felt that God wanted us to have one more child. That door of our hearts had been flung open wide. Now the shocking reality set in, and we knew that gift had never been real. But the trouble was we "felt" it was real. Dwight had already become excited about a new little one, maybe a boy this time. I had felt pregnant, and it seemed my body was already changing, and it was wonderful.

There had not been a baby at all. But I felt like I had lost a child. I felt like the baby I was already longing to hold in my arms was now dead. And I began to grieve.

This was the silent struggle due to the intense longing that began from that counterfeit loss and was a growing a constantly consuming fire on the inside of me. It was with me all day, every day. Although it was nothing like the grief I would experience years later when our precious Tracy died, at the time, it was grief like I had not known before. I could not get rid of it and could not silence it.

At the time, I held this secret inside me. I think I felt embarrassed at a depth of devastation I felt about this and didn't think anyone would understand. It was real, and at the time, I did not recognize it as an attack from my adversary, the devil, who was still trying to destroy our family.

During the weeks and months that followed, I was being constantly tormented. Daily I asked God for a miracle that would allow us to conceive again, but no answer came, and I was caught in the spiral of the "why" questions. I had not yet learned my true identity in Christ, so I did not have that strength to stand upon. I was "blindsided" by the enemy. He loves to trick us, always with a hideous goal to kill and destroy us from the inside out.

One Sunday morning, I woke up with beautiful sunshine streaming in the windows of our bedroom. Dwight was still asleep beside me, and it was in that usually peaceful moment before the family awakes and the house is still. The house was quiet, but as soon as I was awake, my mind began the roller-coaster of emotions. "I want a baby so bad. Now I can't ever have another baby. Oh, how I wish I could have another baby!" Over and over, the waves of sorrow crashed around me.

Suddenly, on that lovely sunny morning with my dear husband laying asleep beside me, Satan spoke to me. I could not hear him with my ears, but there was no doubt it was the evil one who was speaking to my inner self. Very clearly, he said, "Just say yes to me, and you can have another baby."

I froze. I couldn't breathe. The evil was so close. I had no temptation whatsoever to say yes to him. In that instant, I knew the horrors that would bring into our lives. There was no decision to wrestle with. My immediate and absolute response in my heart was, "No!" I did not speak my response out loud because I didn't even want to acknowledge him with a word. In James 4:7-8, we read, "Resist the Devil, and he will flee from you. Come close to God, and God will come close to you" (NLT).

I resisted immediately and totally drew close to God, and in His infinite love and tenderness, God drew close to me. At that moment, God's presence banished that tormenting spirit from me, and I was freed. It was not long after that I realized my heart had been healed. I no longer walked around as if wearing an invisible shroud of grief. God took the counterfeit loss and replaced it with a real presence of Himself that brought joy and peace back into every part of my life. I was again able to walk in freedom, thanking God for the healing He brought to my heart.

Years later, I was able to call upon that deep understanding of loss when I assisted a dear friend in the birth of her still-born baby. She and her husband had already gone through several miscarriages, and this pregnancy had looked so promising. She was about five or six months along when they realized the baby had died. It was devastating for both her and her husband, and she asked if I would come and be with her at the hospital for the still birth. The hours during labor and delivery were somber because we both knew the pains of birth would not lead to joy but to sorrow. There would be no joyous exclamations at the sight of a newborn baby, so pink and soft and wonderful. When the moment of birth came, we saw a perfectly formed baby boy, but his little body had no life in it. God in His mercy was there with us both as we held each other and prayed together through our tears. A perfect little boy was added to heaven's numbers.

There are countless stories I could tell, and memories recalled about those first few years of walking the Spirit-filled life. We sought out conferences, prayer meetings, and anywhere we could learn more about this amazing walk with Jesus. We were blessed to witness how God showed Himself powerful during times of prayer and while ministering to others. We had rich times of growth, of learning who God was and who God was for us. Thankfully, from that day to this, we have never stopped growing in God and learning from Him.

Let me tell you about a group of people we came to know who greatly impacted our lives during that season of time. We have wonderful memories of those relationships even today because we see how God used them to broaden our understanding of many types of people who were different from us and wholly accepted by God. Not far from where we lived in central Minnesota, there had been a hippy commune of some renown throughout the region that had grown to become quite large. Over the years, stories of drugs and drunken orgies had shocked the people living in the surrounding farming communities. During that time, there was a certain older man living in the town near this commune who was full of the Holy Spirit and God's love. He was a Spirit-filled Catholic man who had allowed his heart to be nudged by God to show love to these hippies, who were feared and looked down upon by most everyone else. Dwight and I felt blessed to get to know him and to learn his assignment from the Lord was not to preach at the young people living there but to just love them with the love of Jesus. He would bring them food during the day, often going out during the cold nights of those frigid Minnesota winters and dragging young people out of the snowdrifts where they had passed out from drugs or drink into the safety of warm shelter.

Over many months of showing this kind of unconditional love, the culture of the commune began to change. The young people started asking him why he kept showing them love, and many responded by accepting Jesus Christ as their Lord and Savior. The ones who did not accept Jesus moved away, leaving a wonderful group of young born-again believers.

These people, former hard-core hippies and drug addicts, became our dear friends. They were people who had lived through the hell of addiction and disillusionment with life but who had become radically saved, deeply thankful for what God had done for them.

We had never known people like that before, people who were beautifully real in their love for Jesus and transparent in their relationships with one another. Through countless hours of conversation and Bible study together in a simple farmhouse drinking tea out of Mason jars, or praising God together in a spirit of beautiful worship, our lives were impacted deeply and permanently.

Amazing days of discovery—learning who God was and who He was for us.

Thoughts to ponder

• Think about the people very different from you or your lifestyle, or unexpected circumstances God has brought into your life. How have they changed your relationship with Him?
• Has God shown His light on areas in your past that you feel He wants to change but that you have not fully pursued? Now is the time!

CHAPTER 5:

Called to Follow God's Mission Field ~ 1978

It was now 1978, and we had been managing my father's grocery store for about six years. My dad loved the Lord, but he was struggling with the drastic changes in Dwight's character, which were better but very different. At times it had been difficult for both of them. Dad was a good man with a soft heart who loved God and his family. He and Dwight loved each other and found new ground for their relationship.

We had a good life in that little town of Browerville. It was like a dream come true for me to be living near my parents as well as my extended family. My parents fiercely loved us and their granddaughters, and we had fully expected to follow the plan my dad had set for the business leading to some point when he would sell the grocery story to us and retire. But as time went on, we saw that dad was not nearly ready to make that step. Dwight and I began to strongly feel the need to get out on our own to find the path God had prepared for us. Little did we know that path would lead us back to Washington State.

It was excruciating to tell my parents we were quitting our work with them at the grocery store and even more heartbreaking when, some months later, we announced we were moving back to Washington. Dwight's father was in ill health, and we both had been feeling the pull to return to the Seattle area.

As I wrote earlier, I had first moved to Seattle in 1969 when Dwight was preparing to deploy for his last tour of duty before getting out of the Navy. He had helped me pack my big old Chrysler with all my belongings and drive from southern California to Washington, where I lived at first with his brother Dave and wife before finding a job and small apartment on Queen Anne Hill in Seattle.

So now, in late 1979, after much prayer asking God to give us His wisdom and direction, it seemed the Lord was leading us back to Washington. Although Dwight and I were in unity about the decision, it was a very difficult one for me. Not only my parents, but my sister and her husband, toddler son and newborn twins, aunts and uncles and cousins, all lived in Minnesota. Moving back to Washington meant leaving my whole family. I can remember an afternoon sitting at my mom's kitchen table, again explaining through my tears—probably trying to convince myself as much as her—why we were moving back to Washington. I remember telling my mom that I felt like God was calling me to the mission field. I had no way of knowing that was a prophetic declaration.

We did make the move and, after a couple of "fits and starts," found jobs and were settled in a rental home. Dwight was working on starting his own food service route, delivering meats, cheeses, and deli items to grocery stores. There were some very lean times, and often I would remind God that we were following His leading. If you need to know how many types of meals you can concoct using bologna, I'm your girl!

Finally, we were pretty well settled in jobs that were paying the bills; our daughters were in school and doing fine. I was working for a small manufacturing company and was second in a two-girl office. I was doing okay in my job but could see signs that the business itself was not doing so well, which made for a tense working environment at times.

One Sunday after church, I was visiting with a friend as we walked to our cars in the parking lot. In our conversation, she said something about "the Aglow office." I stopped her. "The Aglow office? What do you mean?"

I had attended Aglow meetings in Alexandria, Minnesota, forty-five miles from where we had lived in Browerville. I loved the freedom in worship, the rich teaching, and the uplifting fellowship with other Spirit-filled women. But I had never even wondered about a home office of the ministry.

My friend told me the headquarter office of Aglow International—known in those days as Women's Aglow Fellowship—was just a few miles away from where we were standing!

In a moment, I decided that was where I wanted to work, spend my time, and where I wanted to use my life in serving the Lord. I did not know it then, but I was on the verge of stepping into that mission field I spoke about with my mom at her kitchen table before leaving Minnesota.

The very next day, I phoned the Aglow office and was invited to make an appointment to come in to fill out an application, followed by a short interview. There were no job openings at the moment, but I was encouraged to phone as often as I liked to inquire about job possibilities.

Through my job hunting experience over the years, I had learned that the one who seems most eager for the job has the best chance of getting hired. In the past, I had landed more than one job using that philosophy, and there had been no other place that I had wanted to work more than I did now at the offices of Aglow!

Wanting to be professional while walking the thin line of showing eager persistence but not being a nuisance, I didn't phone every day. Only several times a week! The woman who answered the phone was always friendly and had come to recognize my voice when I called.

Several weeks went by with no news of job openings at Aglow. During this time, there were growing signs that the business where I was working was having serious problems. One day I arrived at work to learn that fully half of the employees were being laid off. Since I was second in our two-girl office, that meant I was going to be laid off too.

When I left my bosses' office after learning this news, I went straight to the phone on my desk. Sorry to say my first call was not to my husband, but yes, to the Aglow office.

I phoned the Aglow office and spoke to the friendly woman whom I had spoken to many times before. I told her I had just been laid off, and if there were any openings at all, I was available to start work "tomorrow." I was told there actually was a temporary job starting tomorrow! She explained there were other women they usually contacted for these temporary positions, but since I had been calling so often (See, it worked!), perhaps I would like the job. Then I called my husband!

"Do not despise these small beginnings, for the Lord rejoices to see the work begin" (Zechariah 4:10, NLT).

So it was in April of 1980, with great anticipation of what God had prepared for me, that I arrived at the Worldwide Headquarters of Aglow International. I learned that my temporary position was in the Circulation Department, and I would be filing IBM cards in preparation for the next printing of the mailing labels for the upcoming Aglow magazine. In those days, the very popular Aglow magazine was produced by the staff in the Publications Department there, at the Aglow headquarters. After printing, thousands of copies were distributed every other month all around the world. The book published in 2017 by Aglow International and titled *Aglow: The First Fifty Years* states that by 1983 Aglow had produced 75,000 copies of the magazine.

Computers were not yet standard equipment in 1980, and our office was equipped with state-of-the-art electric typewriters! The staff in the Circulation Department was responsible for processing new or changed addresses for the more than 10,000 magazine subscribers, with every name and address typed on a paper IBM card using those electric typewriters. Most subscribers were from the US, but Aglow was quickly growing as an international ministry, so there were also some addresses from other nations.

Before the labels could be printed for the magazine mailing, all of the IBM address cards had to be filed in a certain order, called "clubbing." It was a simple process but also quite exacting. Very basically, it was organizing the cards in zip code order and by name alphabetically within each zip code—all done by hand.

The staff in the Circulation Department had been so busy processing new magazine subscriptions and changes of address they had fallen behind in filing the address cards in the large bins sized to hold the thousands of subscription address cards. They all needed to be accurately filed before the next run of mailing labels could be printed.

So, in the wonderful environment of the Aglow headquarter offices, I began to file address cards. I happily worked at those card bins eight hours a day, and when I was alone during bathroom breaks, I prayed through my tears, pleading with God to make a place for me there after this temporary job was finished.

After about two weeks of filing cards every day, the supervisor of the Circulation Department asked to speak with me. She explained that she was planning to change jobs, and a replacement was needed for her position. They had advertised the job among the others on staff, but no one wanted to work with "all those cards!" So they wondered if I might be willing to do the job. Of course, my answer was "Yes!"

God had answered my prayer. I suddenly went from being a temporary employee doing a short-term project to being supervisor of the Circulation Department!

I was so grateful for what God had done for me and felt I was in full-time ministry. As I worked with all those magazine subscriptions and names of women from all over the United States and even other nations, I saw there were women who lived in inner cities, small towns, rural areas, and everywhere in between. As I looked at each name and address, I wondered what her life was like.

Was there an Aglow fellowship group meeting nearby that she could be part of? Was she part of a church where she could worship God freely and enjoy the friendship and encouragement of other Christian women? Or did she live in a spiritually dry, remote area with this magazine subscription her only link to be able to read Holy Spirit-filled stories and testimonies to encourage her in her walk with God? I loved the work God had given me to do.

After about a year and a half in the Circulation Department, I was asked to interview in the "Foreign Fellowships" Department, later renamed the International Fellowships Department. In 1982, I was hired for the position of assistant to the director, and for the next seventeen years, I was in that position, serving under two directors, Gloria Bistline and then Elaine Keith. I was blessed in countless ways working under those two wonderful women. They taught me godly leadership principles, the value and joy of clear communication, and how to work closely with people from other cultures. When Elaine retired and returned to her home state of Ohio, I was asked to step into the role of director.

Let me jump ahead in my story for a moment to finish this sharing about Aglow.

In 1998, I began serving as executive director of Global Field Offices for Aglow International. I was privileged to work closely with Aglow's International president, Jane Hansen Hoyt, and especially enjoyed the times when we could travel to other nations together. Her wisdom, the depth of her walk with the Lord, and how she shares the gifts of the Spirit with all those around her have profoundly affected who I became and who I am today.

For the next twenty-plus years, I traveled to more than sixty nations, many of those nations multiple times. I so enjoyed the work God had given me to do—working alongside, training, and bringing encouragement to Aglow leaders around the world. When I first began to serve in the International Fellowships Department, Aglow was established in twenty-six nations. By the early 2000s, we were established in 170 nations, so you can imagine how busy those years of growth had been!

Most years, I made six to seven international trips, sometimes visiting several continents during the year. I generally traveled alone to each destination but was met by the national Aglow leaders in that country. All were amazing women who I came to know well and loved like family. When people would ask what I did at Aglow, I would respond, "I attend Aglow meetings with dear friends a long way from home!" The stories about those years of constant travel for Aglow could certainly fill another book!

Those were busy years. In the midst of all the traveling I was doing, which seemed to increase every year, our family was changing. In 1985, Dwight's father died unexpectedly at the age of sixty-two, and our first grandchild was born. (Now, in 2021, we have nine grandchildren and thirteen great-grandchildren!) Terry and Toni were becoming adults and beginning lives of their own. Our relationship with them through the years has often been difficult as they had struggled with invisible scars buried deep from things that happened when they both were too young to remember. But damage was done nonetheless. As I have already shared, their mother had abandoned them both emotionally and physically, leaving them totally alone when Toni was still an infant and Terry a toddler, during times when Dwight was serving aboard ship in the Navy. That abandonment and lack of nurturing had resulted in neglect that would today be called PTSD.

They were both so cute and seemed happy when they were young, but behavior problems would surface throughout their lives at the most unexpected times. I have always called them my daughters, and they called me Mommy/Mom. I believed that if I just loved them enough, I could erase the pain that was buried inside of them. We prayed, bound, and cast off, everything we knew to do. That hurt was so deep and has sadly affected many relationships throughout their lives.

I have a needlepoint picture hanging on the wall in our home that states, "Families are forever." My oldest daughter, Terry, stitched it for me, and I cherish it as a tangible reminder of God's love and perfect plan for us. I believe that little promise with all my heart and cling to hope that all relationships will one day be whole.

There have been good times, but very difficult times as well. How many of you who are reading this can relate? But our journey continues. And we never give up on our kids!

Back to 1988 and the next chapter of our journey.

Thoughts to ponder

- Do you believe God has a plan for your life?
- How long are you willing to wait for Him to bring about His plans for you and your family?
- Are you holding on to hurts, disappointments, or memories of poor choices that are keeping you from experiencing God's love?

CHAPTER 6:

Unexpected Journey ~ 1988

Life was good. I was very busy with my work at Aglow and beginning to travel more to the nations, training and working with the Aglow leaders. We had bought a new home, Terry and Toni were out on their own, and their families were growing, so Tracy was the only one left in the "nest." She was a delightful fourteen-year-old girl who loved us and loved Jesus.

Dwight was only forty-one years old, a hard worker, and in good health. It was hunting season, so most weekends, he spent in the woods searching for those elusive deer. We had no way of knowing about the storm that was brewing.

One day in the fall of 1988, Dwight suddenly developed a pain in his abdomen that sent him first to our doctor, then a few days later to the hospital emergency room. The doctors could not find any cause for the pain, which was growing more intense by the day until he could no longer function. After several trips to the ER, he was finally admitted to the hospital.

Over the next long and excruciating month, the doctors and specialists did every kind of test you can imagine looking for the cause of the incessant and worsening pain. X-rays revealed nothing and, although a big concern was that he had no bowel tones, in other "scope" tests, the doctors could find no reason for the problem.

They connected him to an IV pump that let him administer his own "bump" of pain meds when needed. He couldn't sleep due to the intense pain, so one night, I sat by his bed all night long watching the clock so I could push the button for him at the allowed intervals so he could hopefully get some comfort and much-needed rest. He seemed to sleep all night, and I was thankful—only to learn the next morning that the pump was not functioning properly, and he wasn't receiving any pain meds at all. He had passed out from the pain and had laid there unconscious!

Day after day, I got Tracy off to school and went to spend the day at the hospital. I would wait nervously for each new doctor visit or test result and would stay late into the evening, only to drive home and fall to my knees by the bed praying for God to give us answers.

Our daughter Toni and her husband were staying at our home temporarily, so I was thankful they were there for Tracy during those long evenings when I was at the hospital. Toni had just given birth to their first baby, beautiful Megan, who was born at the same hospital where Dwight was a patient. That was a busy day for me, going between both Toni and Dwight's rooms wanting to be with them both at once!

It had been about a month since Dwight was admitted to the hospital. He had been examined by so many specialists, but no one had any answers to diagnose his deteriorating condition. I was told he was seen by every specialist except maternity!

I was scared, and I was tired. Was God hearing our prayers? Some days I went into the Aglow office to catch up with some things at my desk and talk to my co-workers. They all were praying for Dwight and me and released me to spend most days at the hospital.

One morning I arrived at the hospital as usual, and as I passed the nurses station, I recognized Dwight's personal belongings on a small rolling cart. When I saw this, I thought it meant that he had died and they were taking his things out of the room!

I hurried to his room to find he was still alive, but two nurses were there preparing to move him into the intensive care ward. When I reached the room, they were struggling to transfer him from the bedside hospital recliner into the bed, made very difficult because he had no strength at all to help them. The nurse told me they had called the doctor because they could see Dwight was dying, and the doctor told them to immediately begin preparations for exploratory surgery.

Prior to this, the doctors had not wanted to do surgery because they could not determine that surgery would help. They didn't know what they would be looking for, and with him being so sick, they didn't want to make him heal from an abdominal incision on top of everything else, not knowing if it would reveal the cause of his illness or not.

All the tests that had been administered to try to find the cause of this mysterious illness had proven nothing. A major concern was his digestive system not functioning, so he was not able to swallow any food and water. But nothing had been found to explain the cause of these symptoms.

I followed his bed as they wheeled him into the intensive care unit—ICU. An oxygen mask was fitted to his face, which filled the room with the loud sounds of life-giving air flowing into his lungs. Dwight was too weak to raise his head or even an arm, and as he tried to speak to me, I had to put my ear right against the oxygen mask to hear the words he was trying to say. He was conscious, but his words were incoherent.

In just a few minutes, a doctor entered the room, telling us he needed to explain the dangers of the surgery they were preparing to do. In the middle of this dire explanation, Dwight suddenly sat up in bed and spoke clearly to the doctor!

Moments before, he could barely move or speak. Suddenly he was sitting up in bed speaking strongly enough to be heard over the loud sounds of the oxygen pump.

Dwight interrupted the doctor's explanation of the dangers of surgery and delivered a most amazing speech. He said, "Doctor, I'm not afraid to die! My faith is not here on earth. My faith is in heaven because Jesus Christ is my personal savior. I believe God made good doctors, and that's why I'm here. But my faith is not here on earth. I am not afraid to die!" With that, he slumped back on the bed, as weak as before this amazing outburst.

Visibly shaken, the doctor mumbled a few more words then left the room. Dwight had made his proclamation, and I had my assignment. We would storm heaven for God's will to be done in Dwight's body!

Weeks later, when I told Dwight about what he had proclaimed, he wept. At that moment of being so close to death, he had proclaimed his faith. That was what was on the inside of him, and Jesus was there to hear the declaration of his faith.

After they took Dwight away for surgery, I went to the telephone and began phoning our family and friends, giving them the prayer assignment. Peace surrounded me as I waited, knowing our loved ones were fighting the battle in prayer for us.

Late that night, when they wheeled Dwight back into his room after the surgery, he was on a ventilator, unconscious. They had opened his abdomen "from stem to stern," as they say, searching for the source of what had been threatening to kill him. What they found was shocking. They found gangrene growing in his small intestine. In time, they would learn that small blood clots had formed and, while these grew like snowballs as the blood flowed past, eventually, the circulation was completely blocked, allowing gangrene to set in. That was why he had no bowel tones.

In surgery, the doctors had removed four feet of small intestine, so the gangrene was no longer there, but his whole system was poisoned from that deadly infection that had been growing in his body for the past month. The doctors were doing all they could to keep him alive but in his severely weakened condition had grave doubts he could survive to fight the poison that still threatened his life.

As I stood by Dwight's bed looking at the ominous data blinking across the monitor that he was connected to, the doctor stood next to me, explaining all the numbers and what they hoped would happen through the next twelve hours. This number had to go up, that one decrease, this one remain constant. When he finished, my mind was whirling with it all, and I said, "Doctor, that doesn't even sound possible."

With that, the doctor looked at me in the eye and quietly said, "It is not possible. I'm sorry, but your husband will not live through the night."

But *God* had other plans!

We prayed, and we believed. Dwight did live through that night. And through the next day. And the next night. One day at a time. Eventually, he was strong enough to be moved out of intensive care into a regular hospital room. It would be another month before he was released to go home. During that month, he developed pneumonia which required fluid to be painfully drawn from around his lungs, and more blood clots developed in his legs. After long, difficult weeks, the day finally came when he was released to go home.

Dear one, there are times when we must hang on to the knowledge that we know God has spoken to us even over what we see with our eyes or hear with our ears. I continued to allow the doctors and nurses to medically care for Dwight in all the ways he still needed because I firmly believe God created the medicines and all the amazing knowledge given to doctors. But at the same time, I did not give up the hope and deep faith that God would indeed bring healing to his body. I and those praying with me did not feel it was Dwight's time to die. So, even when the doctor, in the most gentle way possible, predicted that he could not live through the night, it did not destroy my hope.

In times like these, we stand, we believe, and we trust God with both the process and the outcome. As an old hymn says:

> My hope is built on nothing less than Jesus' blood and righteousness; No merit of my own I claim, but wholly lean on Jesus' name. On Christ, the solid rock, I stand; All other ground is sinking sand, All other ground is sinking sand.

It was Dwight's forty-second birthday, December 16, and he talked his doctors into discharging him a bit earlier than they had actually planned. He had been in the hospital since early November, and he wanted to go home! Our daughters had prepared a big banner for his homecoming, excited to have us both home again. I helped him out of the car into the house, and he fell into his recliner, bursting into tears. It had been a long road, with many times not knowing if he would ever be sitting in his living room again.

It took some time to fully recover to regain his strength. We had to make frequent trips to the hospital to have his blood tested so the blood-thinning medication could be properly dosed. It had to be exact because we did not want any more blood clots to form! At first, he was too weak to walk unaided, so he held on to my shoulders as we slowly descended the stairs out of our home to walk to the car. Over the Christmas holiday, he progressed to walking outside all the way to the corner and back. As the New Year of 1989 began, he returned to work.

That began a season of learning to live with a new reality of trusting God for each new day. As time went on and Dwight's gastroenterologist continued seeking the root cause of all these blood clots with their serious complications, some answers emerged.

Dwight was diagnosed with a blood disorder that is now labeled "protein C deficiency." Today it is fairly well known to doctors, but in 1989 it was an emerging science. We were told Dwight was only the third or fourth person in the US to have been diagnosed with this condition. As the years progressed, we had all three of our children tested and urged Dwight's family to get tested too. His mother, one brother, and one nephew were found to have protein C deficiency and began working with their own doctors to take the necessary steps to stay ahead of the effects Dwight had already experienced!

But while Dwight was still recovering, dangerous clotting had silently continued to develop inside his body. Testing eventually revealed that the portal vein to his liver had become completely blocked due to clots that had formed growing inside that large vein until the normal blood flow through that vital organ had been completely stopped. But God, in His wondrous creation of human bodies, had created the way for blood to find new routes so that circulation would continue. God's amazing design had been doing its good work in Dwight's body.

But a problem was also developing when the blood flow through the large portal vein was now being redirected through many small veins. It was as if the strong flow of the big "river" was now redirected through a series of small "streams," and those streams were strained, constantly threatening to break through the barriers overflowing their banks.

Normally, when this happens in a person's body, the doctors just keep an eye on the affected area, prepared to deal with the slim possibility that those smaller veins would "breakthrough" causing an internal bleed. Of course, anyone living with this possibility would know to never take any medication that could thin the blood. Certainly not any kind of prescribed blood thinner!

Dwight's blood flow had redirected itself like it should, which resulted in varicose veins forming in his esophagus and upper part of his stomach. This relieved the pressures in his abdomen but also put him at high risk for bleeding. If these varicose veins would rupture or be torn in any way by foods he ate (swallowing a little fishbone could be deadly!), internal bleeding could happen.

Because of the protein C deficiency and the need to guard against clots forming in Dwight's body, a prescribed blood thinner had to be used. This presented a very dangerous climate resulting in us having to explain a number of times during doctor appointments for other matters; why Dwight was taking a blood-thinning medication while living with such a high risk of internal bleeding.

We learned to live with the knowledge that a dangerous bleeding situation could happen at any time. We learned the signs to look for and the foods to stay away from. A normal question at our house whenever Dwight didn't feel quite right was, "What color is your poop?" Life gets very real at times!

Most of all, we learned to put each day in the capable hands of our loving God, the one who had kept Dwight so far. And the one who we trusted with each new day.

We had been victorious in the battle—all praise to God! Life was back on track. Our youngest daughter, Tracy, was fifteen and loved being a teenager. Terry and Toni had homes of their own, and their families were growing. We continued living our lives as we always had—putting the past behind and looking forward.

Thoughts to ponder

- What is your first thought when you feel overtaken by some life circumstance?
- Do you believe God is close to you, even in those unhappy surprises in life?
- Has God spoken a promise to you that you have had to hold on to in the face of huge obstacles? How did God come through for you?

CHAPTER 7:

Unspeakable Loss ~ 1992

Shadow By My Side

Whatever I do, wherever I go,
I always have a friend to help lead me through.
My friend and I hold each other's hands wherever we go.
You may not be able to see my friend, but he's always there.
I talk to him, and he keeps me company. He may not always
answer, that does not mean he's ignoring me; he just keeps
me company in his own way. Because while that shadow is
beside me, I'll never be lonely.
No, he's not an imaginary friend, just a living shadow by
my side. And if you want to, he can be your friend too.
Just ask, and he'll come.

Tracy Ilene Brooks, 1991

The July 1992 newspaper article was a short four paragraphs.
The heading read "Accident victim dies of injuries." How many
parents sitting with their evening newspaper read those few lines
and thought, *Another teen dies in a car accident. How sad. I'm so
glad my kids are safe tonight.*

Countless times since then have I read similar notices and
felt grieved for the parents and the family, knowing too well that
their very long journey was just beginning.

Years ago, there was a family in the church we attended at the time who lost their daughter in a tragic accident. We prayed for the family but didn't see them at church anymore. I remember thinking, "They must be doing fine." But about five years later, I was reading the local newspaper one evening and read about a man, a loving husband, and father who had committed suicide. I thought, *Such a tragic loss for his family. I wonder what drove him to that.* Then I recognized the name. It was the father of that girl who died. *But,* I thought, *that was so long ago. Surely they were "over it" by now.* How little I knew about the depth of grief in the heart of a parent when their child dies.

At this writing, it has been twenty-eight years since we lost our daughter, Tracy, and it finally seems the time to write this chapter.

I had struggled with this because, however close this much-loved daughter and the story of her life and our loss was to my heart, I deeply felt it needed to be more than just an account of her life and her death. Throughout all these years, I, and my husband and our whole family, have found levels of healing, each in our own way. In the prologue at the beginning of this book, I wrote about some of the bereaved mothers I had met along my journey and how I felt blessed to be able to share with them that joy was still possible for them.

Another long-remembered conversation has also been germinating in my heart for years. It was in May of 2010 when Dwight and I were invited to be the speakers at an Aglow retreat in Sequim, Washington. We each spoke a couple of times, and during one of my messages, I spoke about the loss of our daughter, expressing some of the ways God had helped me to allow peace and even joy back into my life.

Whenever I have shared about this, it has always brought someone to speak to me afterward about their own grief or questions about this loss that seems all so wrong. It is supposed to be the parents who get old and die. Their children are to carry on. Not the other way around.

This time I shared was no different. During the break, a woman came and told me about her friend who had lost their wonderful twenty-one-year-old son some years before. He was their firstborn, loving to his parents and family, an exemplary young man. She said her friend had never quit grieving. She could not find any peace and was still so angry that God took her son.

The woman, telling me this, said she knew several families who have lost children who were so loved and so good. She expressed to me the question that has been cried out to a seemingly silent heaven, "Why does this happen, and how can we deal with it?"

There it is, "the *why* question." That answer remains elusive. I'll talk more about that later in this chapter.

Let me tell you about our daughter.

Our youngest daughter, Tracy, was born on the 4th of July, 1974. Every year on her birthday, I told her the whole nation was celebrating just for her! She had grown into a beautiful young woman, looking forward to an exciting plan ahead of her when she graduated from high school in June 1992. She was enrolled at the nearby community college in their theater arts program— another step toward her goal of becoming an actress.

Just a few months before her high school graduation, Tracy had applied for a position with Taproot Road Company, a Seattle-based Christian theater group. On her application, she wrote, "I want to be an actress and glorify God with my acting."

When Tracy was about eight years old, she announced one evening as we sat watching TV in our living room that she wanted to be an actress. She spoke with all the passion her young heart could express, telling us that "for her whole life" she had wanted to act!

I could fill pages telling about the singing and dancing "performances" she put on for us in the living room or wherever someone would stop to watch. Her performance in the high school play brought people in the audience to tears, and she was excited for the opportunity to audition for a Billy Graham film.

She had a unique flair for putting together creative outfits, either when shopping at her favorite store—Value Village—or cutting out some creation with fabric stretched across the kitchen floor while I was trying to cook dinner and sewing it up to wear to school the next day. Her friends would ask her where she got her outfit. "Oh, I got it at VV's," she would say. Or, "I made it myself."

One homemade creation was extra special. There was going to be a semi-formal dance at school, and Tracy wanted me to help her sew a dress for it. And she knew just the "look" she wanted. We went to the fabric store, and she set her heart on a Vogue pattern for a strapless knee-length dress with a sheer swingy overdress with long fitted sleeves and feather boa trim around the bottom! "I'll help you make it, Mom," she said. So, make it we did—French seams, feather boa trim and all! She was excited to wear it to the school dance and looked smashing!

And she had the occasion to wear that dress for another school function a few months later. As part of one of her school classes, the teacher had organized a fashion show which Tracy was excited to be part of it. The girls were instructed to go to a local dress shop to choose two outfits to borrow from the store to wear in the fashion show. Then they were to choose one outfit from their own closet to wear. You can guess which outfit Tracy chose out of her closet!

Tracy had a nice group of good friends, but she wasn't part of the popular crowd at school. Many of the girls in this fashion show were popular girls who didn't know Tracy well. When it came a time in the fashion show for the girls to put on their own personal outfit, and they saw Tracy in this black satin strapless dress with gold glitter dots and the sheer black overdress with the black feather boa trim! They said to her, "You can't wear that! You're supposed to wear one of your own outfits!" Tracy smiled as she told me how she responded to them. She said, "This is mine. My mom and I made it."

When she stepped out into the spotlights on the runway in the school gym, the gold on her dress made it look like it was on fire. I heard people in the audience gasp at the sight. And I watched my daughter walk that runway with her head held high, wearing an amazing dress—and a confident smile.

Tracy modeling the dress I sewed for her

She was a girl of strong character and determination. She overcame several disabilities in her early years. Her feet were malformed as an infant, so she had to wear braces for six months to straighten them. She suffered hearing loss for a number of years and worked to overcome the difficulties that created. She was diagnosed as having dyslexia as a junior in high school—a disability no one had ever detected before. The counselor said she had overcome it on her own—a real statement to Tracy's strength of character.

During her senior year in high school, she worked in the school office and was hired to continue working over the summer after graduation. A woman she worked under at the office wrote a beautiful letter to us after she died. In the letter, she said Tracy was able to organize things quickly and efficiently with little direction. "She built a database and edited the entire Northshore district student population addresses for the new records system the district had begun to use. It was a dull, lengthy chore, but she never wavered until it was finished." Quite a statement about a seventeen-year-old girl.

She was sensitive and loving, going out of her way to help a friend. She was also fiercely non-prejudiced and accepting of everyone for who they were—no questions asked. She and her oldest sister Terry were best friends, and she and her dad had a special bond. Just a couple of days before the accident, Tracy and her dad were working together out in our yard. She had told him about a friend at school who had died not long before and how senseless that seemed to her. As they talked about this, one of the things Dwight told her was that dying was part of living.

But, oh, the dying part is so much harder for those who are left with the loving memories. On that day, we had no idea how soon our lives were about to change forever.

The phone rang in the middle of the night. It was Harborview Hospital, the trauma center hospital in Seattle. All the nurse would tell me, in a very calm voice, was that our daughter Tracy was there, and we needed to come right away. Could we come now? How long would it take us to arrive? No, they could not answer our questions now. They would talk with us when we got to the hospital emergency room. Please come now.

We threw on our clothes, and as we sped down the freeway, I prayed over and over, "Oh God, I speak health to her head, her limbs, her body." I didn't know what to pray, but I was so afraid. When we reached the hospital parking lot and ran to the entrance, my legs felt like wooden pegs. I was in shock.

Just hours before, I had talked to her on the phone. She said she was going to her best friend Keith's house to watch a movie after work. She told me about her day at the office of the high school. She had gotten a paper cut on her finger that hurt, and she had to wear a band-aid. I told her I was altering the sleeves on the dress we had bought for her to wear at her sister's upcoming wedding. It was the dress she wore when we buried her.

When we arrived at Harborview, they ushered us into a small private waiting room. No one had any information for us. What happened? How badly was she injured? Can we see her? Where did it happen? "A doctor will be here soon to talk with you," was all we were told.

I don't know how long we waited. It seemed like hours. Finally, a doctor came to talk with us. We learned she had been in a car accident and was gravely injured. Her neck was broken, and she was not conscious. She had been brought to Harborview trauma center by medical helicopter but had not regained consciousness, and she was on life support. We would be brought to see her soon, but her condition was grave.

I listened, dry-eyed. What were they saying about my daughter? My mind could not comprehend what they were telling me.

We had to wait for several hours before we could see her. During those hours, we began to call our family, close friends, and colleagues at our workplaces. The most dreaded call was to my parents. I couldn't bear the pain they would feel. They had been at our home for several weeks over Tracy's high school graduation, having only returned to their home in Minnesota a few days before. I wept as I told them the little we knew at that point but that our Tracy was gravely hurt, and yes, they probably should come quickly.

Both my mom and dad had a very close relationship with Tracy. Every year since we had moved from Minnesota back to Washington, Tracy had spent the entire summers with them, and they both loved her with pride and a joy that was a delight to witness.

Finally, we were brought to our daughter's hospital room in the intensive care ward. She had a "halo" encircling her head to stabilize her broken neck, and the only sound in the room was the ventilator with its rhythmic sound pumping air into her lungs. I looked at her with a strange sense of detachment. I couldn't fully comprehend the sight. I touched her skin, and it was warm. Her hair smelled sweetly of her shampoo. I saw the Band-Aid on her finger and remembered the paper cut she had told me about on the phone just hours before when we talked for what would be the last time. I gently pulled off the Band-Aid and noticed the paper cut was already starting to heal.

My mind could not comprehend the reality of the situation.

We learned that she had ridden with two friends over to Keith's house, and they had all watched a movie together on TV. After the movie, her friends were driving her back to where she had left her car. She was sitting in the back seat on the passenger side, with her lap seat belt fastened. It was a dry summer evening, there was no traffic, and they were not speeding. We believe the driver looked over his right shoulder to say something to Tracy in the back seat and, in that movement, turned the wheel to the right. In a moment, the car veered off the road over the curb and through a shallow ditch, hitting a small tree on the other side of the ditch. The two friends in the front seat were not wearing their seat belts and hit their heads on the windshield but were not badly injured. In the back seat, the action of the car going through the ditch and immediately hitting the tree caused Tracy to suffer a devastating whiplash that broke her neck high at the third vertebrae. There were no lacerations on her body. The police later told us they had never seen a car damaged so little in an accident where someone died.

The next three days in the ICU ward of the hospital were a blur. Family arrived, friends and co-workers came and went. Someone brought food to us, we waited, and we prayed.

When we were allowed to go into her room for short periods of time, we stood beside her bed and prayed for God to touch her. We were so filled with faith and the absolute belief that she would be healed. Even as she lay there with that hardware drilled into her skull and the ventilator tube breathing for her, I was expecting and believing she would suddenly open her eyes and be healed.

We could feel God's presence in that room. As I stood beside her bed with my eyes closed in prayer, I could "see" two sets of angel wings hovering over her body, and I could "feel" the wind from their wings on my skin. From that day to this, that vision is real to me, and I can vividly remember the feel of that soft heavenly wind.

"He sends his angels like the winds, his servants like flames of fire" (Hebrews 1:7, NLT). And again in Psalm 104:4, "The winds are your messengers" (NLT).

I wanted to believe God sent those angels to carry His healing to my daughter. But now I know they were the angels God sent to hover and wait for the moment they were to escort her soul to heaven.

Throughout that first day, those angels' wings were there, and when Dwight and I were standing by her bedside, we both could feel her presence. Her spirit still inhabited her body, and we could feel her there in the room with us. Very early the next morning, Dwight left the family waiting room where we had been allowed to spend the night, and he went in to see Tracy by himself. When he came back, he offered no explanation but asked me to go with him to her room again. As we entered and stood by her bed, we silently just looked at her and then at one another. We could no longer feel her presence in the room. And I could no longer "see" the angels' wings nor feel their heavenly wind. They had escorted our beautiful daughter to heaven, into the presence of Jesus, Who met her there with arms of love open wide to receive her.

Just four short years before, I had stood next to my husband's bed listening to a doctor telling me he could not live through the night. But that night, I somehow knew his outcome would not be death. God gave me the faith to believe and to hang on to His promise.

But this time, it was different. God was there. His presence surrounding us was as real as the feeling of being submerged in warm water, safe and secure in an atmosphere of His loving care. But I had no promise in my heart that she would live and not die. I surely prayed that and, with everything in me, wanted it to be true. But in that tangible holy presence, I was also being baptized into a new journey that was the most difficult thing I have ever experienced.

Do I think God caused the accident? No, I do not. I believe, sadly, that accidents happen. Accidents happen to bad people and to good people. This time it happened to us.

I also believe God has a plan for each of us as His children and a day of His choosing when He will bring us to our heavenly home. We are to live our lives fully, with every expectation that we will live to a ripe old age. But, for reasons I trust to my heavenly Father who loves me completely, that is not always so. It was not to be so for my daughter, who fulfilled her journey on earth in eighteen years and fourteen days.

Although her spirit had left her body, the life support was keeping her organs functioning. Her skin was still warm when I touched her, and even the sweet smell of shampoo was still in her hair.

After three days at the hospital, the nurses finally convinced Dwight and me to go home and get some rest. Leaving the hospital that day was utter anguish. We slowly walked to the elevator and hesitated before pushing the button to take us down to the ground floor. We forced ourselves to walk out the door into the sunshine, but our hearts were still up in that room. We walked to our car, and we both just stood and looked at each other over the hood of the car with tears streaming down our faces. No words. Only the deepest sorrow.

We kept in close contact by phone with the hospital. The next day we finally had to make the unspeakable decision to remove her life support. Her internal organs were under great stress from the high level of life support that was needed, and the medical personnel gently assured us it was the right decision. We knew her spirit was no longer in her body, but oh, how we loved that body that had been our precious daughter.

Our close friends Ivan and Helen came to our house so Helen could stay with our parents while Ivan drove us to the hospital. He stayed outside while we went in.

The four of us, Dwight and I, Terry and Toni, were brought into the room where they had moved her on that last day to say our final goodbyes. I remember it as a larger space, and there was another bed with a young woman in it at the far end of the room. I stood near Tracy's bed, dry-eyed, just watching this scene that my mind would not comprehend. Toni was standing at the foot of the bed, crying silently. Terry was overcome with emotion and was screaming "My sister, my sister" over and over until she fainted. Dwight was helping to get her safely lowered into a chair while a nurse was running for smelling salts. And I just stood there, watching these impossible things happening around me.

It was at that moment, in the midst of all this tragic chaos, I heard the voice of a nurse at the bedside of the young woman at the far side of the room. Just then, that young woman was waking up from a coma, and the nurse was gaily speaking to her to help her fully awaken. It was surreal.

We were surrounded by loving family and friends who helped us in any way they could or in any way we would allow them to. Dwight and I were hurting so deeply that we found ourselves trying to shield others who were actually hurting as badly as we were. Neither of us was thinking correctly at that point.

On the day we went to the funeral home to plan her service and pick out her casket, Dwight and I insisted on going alone, just the two of us. Looking back, that was not wisdom, but the grief our parents were carrying—for us as well as for losing their granddaughter—was overwhelming. Today it is a comfort to know they are together in heaven.

We somehow planned the funeral service and the visitation that was held the evening before. I am almost embarrassed to remember that evening as I tried to be the "hostess," making sure everyone was alright and feeling cared for. I knew how to do that! I did not know how to grieve losing my daughter!

For the funeral, we asked that a song be sung that had been performed by the youth "Fire Choir" that Tracy was part of, "Our God is an Awesome God." My Aglow sisters came to our home during the funeral and prepared lunch for all who gathered afterward. I remember talking to people, even smiling at times, assuring everyone we would be okay and God was in control.

Yes, God indeed is awesome. His presence and strength were holding me up even when I had no idea how to act, what to say, who I was anymore.

A comforting memory is of the ones who were able to spend some days with us in our home after all the busyness surrounding the funeral. Our dear parents, Dwight's brother and his wife, our daughters, and dear cousin, Shirley, who had come up from California to spend that tender time with us. I especially remember one afternoon when we all sat around our dining room table with a huge stack of sympathy cards that had arrived from near and far. It was amazing to see postmarks from many nations, cards sent by Aglow leaders around the world. As we sat around the table, we took turns reading cards. When one began to cry too much to read any further, the next one would take over—the comfort of sharing tears together.

I have always considered myself to be a person who met life in realistic terms. I had never been overly emotional and was generally even-tempered and calm. So, if anyone would have told me during the days and weeks after the funeral that I was in denial, I would have disagreed with them. I was crying, and I was talking about Tracy and communicating with Dwight and those around me. I knew painfully well what had happened!

But it was a full two months after her death when, on a sunny afternoon at home, I was wiping the counter in my kitchen when suddenly my whole body jolted, and I thought, *She's dead.* Throughout the rest of that day, every few moments, my body shook, and I realized again, *She's dead. Oh, she's really dead.* The full realization had been too awful, too impossible, and in involuntary self-protection, I had been in denial. God had given me that buffer as He was caring for me. That day the real grief began.

I cried and wept for hours every day. When I started going back to the Aglow office, I sometimes could not make it through the whole day and sometimes started the drive but, partway down the freeway, had to turn around and come home again. Mountains of wet tissues grew wherever I was sitting. The tears flowed from the depth of my heart that I could not even fathom.

My heart was not angry. It was just so incredibly sad and missing my daughter. I was heartbroken for myself and everyone around me who was grieving her loss. Why had this happened to her and to us?

Dwight suffered in his own way. He became mad at God for taking his daughter. He cried, "God, why didn't you take me instead?" Morning after morning, I would listen to him wail in anguished cries while he was in the shower. He was heartbroken too.

Five years went by, and Dwight would not go to church or have any relationship with God. But a day came when God spoke to Dwight's heart that He wanted him to come to the Aglow conference. That year, 1997, it was going to be in New Orleans, and he could not get time off work, so it was no small effort or expense for him to travel all the way from Seattle to New Orleans for a short weekend. But we made plans for him to join me in New Orleans, arriving late on Friday night and staying until Sunday morning. I was so proud of Dwight for hearing—and heeding—God's word to him. It seemed God would surely have a wonderful purpose in it all.

It was Dwight's first experience at an Aglow conference, and it was the first time he had seen me working "in my element." When he arrived at the convention center to meet me for dinner before the opening session, I was still in rehearsal for the flag parade, directing the hundred-plus women from all over the world. All were wearing their national dress, and it is quite an impressive sight. While I finished the rehearsal, he stood back and just watched me. When I finally saw him walking toward me, he was looking at me as if he had never seen me before! I had no idea that God was changing many things in our relationship that weekend.

I was stage manager for the conference that year, so I had a perfect view of where Dwight was sitting in the second row, right in front of the stage. During the worship time in the opening conference session, I saw tears begin to fall from Dwight's eyes and then saw his hands raised in worship. He told me later that God spoke to his heart, saying, "Aren't you tired of being mad at Me?" Dwight responded, "Yes, God, it's a lot of work to stay mad at You."

That began the healing of Dwight's heart and led to many opened doors for Dwight to minister healing and deliverance to others. God's love never ends for us, and His timing is perfect.

⁓⋇⁓

In preparation for writing this chapter, I went through all the journals I had kept for about the first five years after our daughter's death. In those years, writing in my journal became my place of refuge, my lifeline—pages filled with heart-wrenching descriptions of my thoughts, memories, and feelings of the moment. Painfully I described feeling as though my body was bloodied and torn, with no remedy or relief. And other pages filled with words of comfort that I had read somewhere or that had come out of a conversation with Dwight. Thankfully, we never stopped talking with each other. We often talked about the same memories, or hurts, or dreams over and over, as if we were trying to convince even ourselves these things had really happened.

I was told journaling would help, and I had tried to do everything people told me would be good for me to do, including reading all the books I could about other parents who had lost children. Of course, each family's story was personal and the details different, but I thought if they could live through their experience of the loss of a child, just maybe, I could live through it, too.

At times I wasn't sure, but I desperately wanted to make some kind of sense out of my daughter's death. I never blamed God for the accident, but I so wanted to find some divine reason for it.

I was at my most transparent with God when I was alone in my car. Every evening when I drove into our driveway after work, the passenger seat of my car was covered with wet tissues.

I was desperate to hang on to Jesus because I knew He was my only strength, and I needed Him now more than ever before. But too many of my prayers included my plea to tell me why. Why did my daughter die that night? Why wasn't she healed? Why is she gone from us forever? Why God, why? But God doesn't answer that question.

As I said, I was hanging on to prayer as a lifeline, but finally, one day, my grip was no longer strong enough. I could no longer hang on, even to prayer. Notice it was *my* strength I was counting on then.

In the midst of another soggy prayer session, I began to yell (yes, yell) my frustrations out to God. I had been trying so hard, but my prayers weren't doing any good. God wasn't answering, and probably not even listening! I felt that brass ceiling where my prayers just bounced off and fell useless at my feet. I railed at God in anguish and hurt. I had never talked to Him that way before. As I wore myself out from my tirade, I ended with, "God, I'm done praying! I'm sorry, but You will just have to deal with it!" At that moment, I didn't even care if lightning struck! I was done with praying!

As silence fell in my car, something happened that was so completely unexpected; it could only have been God. I heard clearly in my mind, "Well then, just praise Me."

I was shocked! But I knew it was God. My first thought was, *How could He say that to me in a moment like this! That isn't even very nice!* But my next thought was, *You are God. You loved me enough to speak to my heart just now, so it must be something good for me.* So my response was, "Okay, God, I can do that."

Right there in the car, as my anger melted away into obedience, I began to sing, "This is the day. This is the day. That the

Lord has made. That the Lord has made. I will rejoice and be glad in it" (Psalm 118:24, NLT). I wasn't really feeling glad, but I was walking in the way Jesus was leading me.

For weeks after that, my total prayer life consisted of singing the simple praise choruses I had learned years before. Even "Jesus loves me" was part of my regular repertoire as I followed the loving direction of my Jesus to "just praise Me." And little by little, peace began to invade my heart, and the desperation seemed to be lighter. Pain was still there, but I was giving Him more of it to carry for me.

When sorrow is overwhelming, we can always be honest with God. And when we don't feel like rejoicing, we can tell God how we truly feel. At times like those, God, from His heart of understanding, will give us reason to rejoice. We can become glad in this gift of another day to live and to serve Him.

Praising God is another way of thanking Him for who He is and who He is for us. When we thank Him, it helps us to release our control of the situation—in this case, my control of the grief that was holding me so tightly. What followed was the door of communication beginning to open again. He had not closed it, but in the paralysis of my grief, I had lost my intimacy with Him.

In whatever desperate circumstance you find yourself, do you have difficulty believing God cares, believing He can and will answer prayer, or trusting Him for the circumstances of your life? Your faith will be strengthened if you will start praising God. You don't have to feel like it; just start verbally out loud praising God for who He is and that He loves you—no matter what. That praise will strengthen your faith, and you will find that you can believe God in those areas that were such a struggle before.

I very often use the wonderful daily devotional "My Utmost for His Highest" (Oswald Chambers/Discovery House Publishers) and have found in it precious but also challenging thoughts to ponder. In the entry for April 14, the devotional asks where joy comes from in a person. Some people would say, "Well, they are able to be joyful because their life is easy and they don't have burdens to carry." But Chambers challenges, "Lift the veil. The fact that the peace and the light and the joy of God are there is proof that the burden is there too."

A dear friend, Doris Ott, once reminded me that the veil between this life and the next is very thin. I believe that. We can all say of loved ones who passed through that veil, "They were here, and then they were not." They passed through the veil into their new life of eternal joy in heaven. Oh, how I loved reading people's accounts of heaven after their account of receiving a glimpse into that realm following a traumatic event of some kind. The veil is so thin.

One afternoon shortly after my daughter's funeral, I decided the pain was too great, and for a moment, thought it would be so much easier if I could just pass through that veil. I lay down on our bed and decided I would simply stop breathing. But we know it doesn't work like that. We are called to remain on this earth and to keep on seeking God for His leading, His peace, and direction. And to do that, we must make certain decisions for our lives.

Do we want to hide ourselves away with our pain and draw the curtains against God and people in our lives? Some people do that and, sadly, it is their decision.

In October 1992, three months after my daughter's death, I wrote in my journal, "I made a conscious decision that I do not want to respond to life from now on out of a place of woundedness, but out of restored health in God. I don't want to live my life as 'a woman who has lost a child.' I am that and always will be, but I don't have to view life from that perspective, in a negative way."

My journey back to wholeness was still a long way off; it would be five years to feel I could fully breathe again. But the struggle always kept me facing forward because I had made this decision to find joy again. God's strength is freely available to us whenever we seek Him to find meaning and to go through our days. But we need to employ the strength that He gives to us. Through Him, it is absolutely available. He allows you to make the decision to reach out and take it, and then hold on with both hands to keep it while the fullness of healing comes into your heart and life.

I was so fortunate in being surrounded by many strong, mature Christian friends at Aglow who were always willing to listen to me when I needed to talk and to pray for me. But I have to admit that at times, especially in the early days when my emotions were particularly raw and I wasn't handling anything well, that I wanted to resist receiving prayer. Because inside my mind, I thought, *What will they pray for? That I won't be sad anymore? That I'll forget this pain? What can prayer do to change the circumstance of my loss?* The truth I couldn't really explain to anyone was that I didn't want to be "healed" or to forget any of it. Even the pain was something that connected me to my daughter—warped, yes. But a true emotion.

One day, during a staff prayer time at the Aglow office, I was taken into a vision. I "saw" waves of water, and as I watched, they turned to stone. I became afraid, and I prayed, "God, please don't let my heart become hardened!" Later I found the scripture in 2 Corinthians 3:3 that speaks of a letter "written not with pen and ink, but with the Spirit of the living God. It is carved not on stone, but on human hearts" (NLT).

As I pondered that in my heart, God showed me that waves of grief are like water flowing over and over, with no end. But those waves of grief can be lovingly carved by the Spirit of God, not on stone but on our hearts, so there can be an end to the grief that would want to drown us. Instead, we can look at it and remember. We don't need to forget all the memories, even those that might bring some tears again. But then we can also put those memories away and walk in joy and hope.

Dear one, you can receive true peace, hope, and even joy again. You don't need to lose the memories, but they can be put aside to no longer keep you in despair.

One of the books I read was *Disappointment With God* by Philip Yancey (Zondervan Publishing House). I drew many good things from this book, but a primary truth has stayed with me.

Jesus loves us with a love so personal, so individual, so complete, and in His sacrifice for us, He experienced all our sorrows. Throughout all our life's highs and lows, He cries with us when we are sad, and He rejoices with us when we are happy. But through all of life's journey, through it all, He asks us, "Do you love Me? Will you love Me even now, even through this?"

Our answer must always be, "Yes, Lord, I love You even now."

I am not a trained expert. I don't have all the answers. But I have lived this journey of a devastating loss since July 1992 and can testify that God has been my comforter, healer, and ever-present friend. He has been the living shadow by my side. Wherever your journey has brought you, Jesus is there to comfort you, lead you, and heal your heart.

We often hear people say, "Why do bad things happen to good people?" Like the woman I spoke of near the beginning of this chapter. Why did her beautiful twenty-one-year-old son, who was so good in every way, have to die?

I believe with all my heart that God does not cause these tragedies. He is a good God, and creating that kind of sorrow is not in His nature. But we live in a fallen world. Sometimes, accidents happen to good people, and sometimes to bad people. This time, an accident happened to us.

The only response that brings any shred of salvage to our wounded hearts is, "Okay, God, here I am still standing and still determined to follow You. Please help me, Lord."

One more thought before the journey moves us on.

In 2004, I was in Russia for Aglow. My friend Agneta and I were invited for dinner to the home of a family she knew who lived in a village outside Moscow. The village was quite remote, with small, neat homes lining dirt streets, all built around a large abandoned factory building that was silent proof of a more prosperous past.

It was a lovely family of three generations living in this comfortable Russian home, and as we gathered around their kitchen table, which had been carried out into the back yard where we sat for our dinner, the conversation was bright and interesting. One of the older children spoke good English, so the conversation moved along, and when the elderly grandfather began to speak, I was grateful for the excellent interpretation.

This gentle old man had been a Christian for many years, since long before it was safe to profess your faith in Russia. He had amazing stories to tell and also asked me many questions about my life. So, in the course of our conversation, I told him about the death of my daughter.

His words were gentle and kind and filled with the wisdom of one who had walked with God through many trials and tragedies himself. One of the things that most pierced my heart was when he said to me, "It would be very difficult to tell someone they needed to lose a child to get to the place where God wanted them to be." What did that mean? This old man agreed with me that God did not cause that accident, but God, in His love for me, would bring "beauty for ashes" if I would allow that.

For years I pondered that statement until one day, when I read the entry for November 1 in *My Utmost for His Highest*, the Oswald Chambers devotional I referenced earlier. I encourage you to read that for yourself. It is a little "tough," but as I have pondered those words, it has ministered to me on many levels. It describes just what that elderly Russian man said to me.

"…Why shouldn't we go through heartbreaks? Through those doorways, God is opening up ways of fellowship with His Son … If through a broken heart God can bring His purposes to pass in the world, then thank Him for breaking your heart" (*My Utmost for His Highest* by Oswald Chambers, devotion for November 1).

Thoughts to ponder

- What do you believe your reaction would be to a tragedy in your life?
- Are you struggling with a tragic loss and still cannot accept God's comforting love?
- Do you believe you can choose how you will react emotionally to trials in your life?
- Where are you in your journey to wholeness?

Tracy age seventeen, 1991

CHAPTER 8

More Life Journeys—
Drug Abuse and Breast Cancer ~ 1997 and 2003

> But you, O Lord, are a shield for me; My glory, the One who lifts up my head. I cried to the Lord with my voice, and He heard me from His holy hill. Selah. I lay down and slept; I awoke for the Lord sustained me.
>
> Psalm 3:3-5 (NKJV)

Our Family's Journey through Drug Abuse

I've often used the word "journey" as I have moved through our story. We all are on a journey through life, and the road is seldom straight or level. The next years in the life of my family continued to challenge and stretch us.

Our oldest daughter, Terry, had lost her best friend when her sister Tracy died, and in her grief, she turned to drugs. We were not at all familiar with this type of addiction and had no idea of the signs to watch for. We did not even know where the drug use began. Crack cocaine was her drug of choice. It was a terrible season for her, her children, and our whole family. By the summer of 1998, she had lost her home; her children went to live with our other daughter Toni and her family. After a time out on the streets living the drug lifestyle, Terry finally called me one day while I was at work and reached out for help.

It was August 28, 1998. I had been praying every day that she would quickly reach her "bottom" and be forced to look up. I prayed she would call me, but when the phone at my desk at the Aglow office rang, and I heard her voice, I was still shocked. She was talking very fast and almost in a whisper. She said she was scared that the dangerous people she was with would hear her on the phone and try to stop her from leaving.

She told me later that she was in a house where other people were just hanging out; most were high. Suddenly someone pulled a knife and threatened the young man sitting right next to her on the couch. She thought she was going to be killed. That is what it took for her to make that phone call to me, asking for help. That's what it took for her to reach her bottom.

She said she needed help. She wanted me to pick her up in front of the grocery store on a major intersection located about halfway between the Aglow office and where our home was. She sounded frantic and asked how soon I could get there.

I immediately prepared to leave the office, but not before I had phoned the detox center. I had gathered all the necessary phone numbers, hoping I would have the opportunity to use them if she called me. I quickly explained and asked if I could bring my daughter there. They said yes. They had one bed available.

I drove as fast as I could to the grocery store, where she told me to meet her. I parked, got out of my car, and waited. Where exactly should I be standing so she would see me? I walked to the front of the store, waited a few minutes, then walked back and stood by my car. I didn't want to miss her!

Then I thought, *She said, "meet me at the intersection,"* so I walked to the nearest corner of that busy intersection and, after only a minute or two, saw her about a block away walking toward me down the sidewalk on the opposite side of the street.

She reached the intersection, waited through the stoplight, and crossed when the "walk" sign illuminated. One more red light to wait through at the opposite corner. I couldn't take my eyes off her.

We stood looking at each other from across that busy street, waiting impatiently for the light to turn green. When it did, I ran out into the middle of the street to meet her and to get my arms around her. We both were nervous. She was high on drugs, frantic to get into my car and have me drive her away from there. Even though she had escaped, she was paranoid and still afraid the people from that house would follow her and make her go back.

She relaxed a bit as we put some distance between us and from where she had fled, so I asked if she was hungry. We stopped at a McDonald's, and while she was eating, I carefully told her that I was taking her to the detox center. I didn't know what she was expecting me to do, but I knew Dwight and I were not equipped to give her the real help she needed. First, she had to come down from the high she had likely been on for weeks.

She said, "No, Mom, I called there, and they're all full." But I said, "Well, I just called, and there was one bed left. They're holding it for you."

God had His hand on her, and He was leading her to safety.

She asked me to stop at a drug store to buy some lice shampoo, and from there, we drove straight to the detox center where Terry was checked in. As I left her there, I committed her again to the Lord.

It was not an easy time. The second day at detox, Terry was more herself again and wanted to see her daughters. So we picked them up from our other daughter's home where they were now living and brought them to the detox center so she could see them. It was a tearful reunion as Terry began to realize what she had done. But those tears were the hopeful sign that she was willing to change. After the maximum stay of three days, Dwight and I picked her up and brought her to our home. She didn't try to leave. She wanted help and was afraid to be left alone. She didn't trust herself. She came with me to the office each day, and I even went with her to the bathroom.

We knew all about alcoholism but surely did not have any experience in how to help a drug addict. We didn't even know where to begin, but God led us, step by step, to talk with various counselors and agencies. We were able to arrange for an evaluation and to learn about all the types of help that were available.

We wanted to help our daughter but really could not afford the high cost of many of the treatment plans. We cried out to God to help us know what to do. The social worker assigned to us was a Christian, and just knowing that helped us find peace as we navigated through the decisions we had to help our daughter make.

It was only about two weeks until we were able to get her into a county-run in-patient treatment facility about three hours from where we live. The process of healing began. It was hard work for her, and we were so grateful she was determined to see it through.

At first, she could not have visitors, then finally, we were able to bring her two little daughters to visit her on Sunday afternoons. Those days encouraged her to keep on fighting for wholeness in her life. For Dwight and I, they were poignant reminders of the battle we were walking through.

Seventeen months of inpatient treatment, followed by outpatient treatment, and finally to living in a halfway house. Each step brought her closer to home and closer to being strong enough to live on her own. The day in January 2000 that she moved into her own low-rent apartment, we both stood in that small living room and cried. It had been a long hard journey for us all.

Today I am so grateful to say that she has been drug-free for over twenty-two years and has been able to help other young people struggling with that terrible addiction. She has never had a relapse, for which we are eternally grateful and know there are countless families who go through the process of recovery many times only to face heartache over and over again. But the years of drug abuse took their toll nevertheless in the long-term health of her body.

Terry's story is much longer than this, but I will leave the rest for her to tell herself someday. God in His grace is still by her side every day.

My Journey through Breast Cancer

"Mrs. Brooks, you have breast cancer."

In the early spring of 2003, during my annual routine mammogram, a small lump was detected on the X-ray picture. Neither I nor the doctor could feel it through my skin but, thankfully, the mammogram revealed it. A needle biopsy was taken, and a few days later, I learned the diagnosis was breast cancer. The end of this story is that following lumpectomy surgery and a series of radiation treatments, I was well on my way to full recovery and have been cancer-free ever since. God is so good.

That's the short story. Praise God! But any journey through cancer is a long and emotional one.

When you're told you have breast cancer, all the things you've ever heard or read about other women come crashing like a tidal wave into your mind. The stories you remember are usually those that did not end well. Cancer has happened to so many others. But this time, it is happening to me. What does this mean for the rest of my life, and what will my body look like after I've survived it? I had every intention of surviving this cancer, but I hoped it wouldn't mean I would lose my breast. My faith was strong, and I had seen the power of warring in prayer for my husband. No doubts there. But to be honest, the battle looks a bit different when viewed from the fox hole rather than "command central."

My paternal grandmother had lost both her breasts as a result of two different cancers that had attacked her body, and an aunt had also suffered this experience. There was no cancer on my mother's side of the family, but still, the thoughts were there.

The previous couple of years had been a very busy season of Aglow travel. As mentioned earlier, I had become director of the International Field Office at Aglow, and my responsibilities included working closely with the Aglow national leadership outside the US, which at that time covered well over 150 nations. We developed what grew to be eight regional committees which were made up of some or all of the Aglow national leaders in the continent or region. Prior to this, each nation and its Aglow leadership related directly to Aglow headquarters, and there was not much interaction between nations. A regional committee provided a structured format for the Aglow national presidents to relate and encourage one another as peers, plan conferences together for the Aglow members in all the nations of their Aglow region, and, very importantly, get to know each other. It was all very positive, and all the leaders were motivated to meet together as often as possible, at least once or sometimes twice a year. I was traveling extensively to meet with each committee in their nations to help them adapt guidelines for their particular regional committee that fit their culture and language.

The year before, 2002, I had made four international trips, visiting nine nations in Europe and South America. In 2003, I had already made one international trip with plans set for two more. It was a busy time, and cancer was not in my schedule!

So, in late March, when I received the diagnosis of cancer, I was scheduled to travel to Bolivia just four days later. My oncologist agreed to my traveling out of the country while waiting for my surgery date, and of course, I was surrounded by praying, faith-filled women all during my stay in La Paz.

My surgery was scheduled for the week after I returned home from Bolivia. During that time, I had a couple of days in the Aglow office and felt so blessed when my dear sisters there gathered around me to pray before my surgery date.

Their prayers were filled with faith and declarations of God's power and love for me. They were the kind of prayers that send you off full of strength and courage! God's peace surrounded me throughout those final days of waiting and even when I was in the hospital being prepped for surgery. I told the doctor to take enough tissue to "get it all," and he promised he would do his best. Sentinel node tests had already determined cancer had likely not spread outside the small tumor, and aside from the normal apprehension, I felt confident and at peace.

The initial post-surgery pathology reports were good, and the doctor was confident he "got it all." So, several hours after the surgery, I was discharged from the hospital, feeling grateful to my doctor for ordering me home to spend the week resting in bed and do nothing!

It was a rare thing for me to lie in bed and do nothing, and it gave me time to let my mind wander to wherever God took my thoughts. One scripture that kept coming to me was one that had been prayed over me that day at the Aglow office. It was from Mark 11:23. Jesus is speaking, and He says,

> I tell you the truth, you can say to this mountain,
> "May you be lifted up and thrown into the sea,"
> and it will happen. But you must really believe
> it will happen and have no doubt in your heart.

> Mark 11:23 (NLT)

Doubt is an interesting emotion. It's like a nagging thing disturbing the fringes of our peace. It can even fray our garments of praise and threaten to replace faith with fear.

In any life situation, and certainly in the situation I was experiencing recuperating from cancer surgery and waiting for the final pathology report, doubt is something that lurks around just waiting for attention. "God, I really do believe! I trust You and believe my body is free of cancer!" But how do I stay free from all doubt?

It's like telling a child that if he doesn't stick his tongue in the spot where his tooth has fallen out, a gold tooth will grow there. Were you ever told that as a child by a mischievous childhood friend? The child doesn't know it's only a story, and he determines to have that gold tooth! But then suddenly, before he even realizes he's done it—his tongue is in that empty spot feeling for the new tooth. It has happened, and he can't take it back!

We proclaim, "God, I will not doubt." But suddenly, doubt comes into our minds. It's quick and fleeting, but a doubt nevertheless. So is all hope now dashed, for that one doubt? Heavy questions for a week at home "resting" in bed!

It was Easter week, so I decided to read the passion story in all four of the Gospels. That would be more uplifting than wondering about doubt! But as I read them, I was surprised to find the word "doubt" in all four of those accounts. This led me to do a word study of the word "doubt." And what I discovered freed my heart.

In Mark 11:23, the Greek word for doubt is *diakrino*, pronounced "dee-a-kree-no." This word refers to "doubt in your heart." And actually, the scripture says just that in the New Living Translation; "have no doubt in your heart." Some of the definitions are: to separate thoroughly, to withdraw from, oppose. It means, "I do not believe it! In my heart, I turn away from it and proclaim it not true."

Next, I searched out the word doubt that was used in the other Gospels (Matthew, Luke, and John) and found that it actually was a completely different word in Greek. That word is pronounced "dis-tădzo." This word refers to "doubt in your mind." Some of the definitions are: to waver in opinion, to doubt in our mind. It means: Even though I don't understand this, I still do believe it.

As I read those passionate accounts of the events surrounding Jesus' death on the cross, followed by His resurrection, transfiguration, and finally His ascension, I was amazed to realize that the disciples experienced doubt! They had been eye-witnesses to all the miracles and teachings of Jesus, as well as those awesome events during the last days of His life here on earth. And yet they doubted!

But I realized that their doubt was "distadzo." Their doubt was not "diakrino," meaning they absolutely did not believe. They believed; they just did not understand. In Luke 24, Jesus appears to His disciples for the first time after the crucifixion. Verse forty-one says, "Still they stood there in disbelief, filled with joy and wonder" (NLT). Even in the midst of their joy, the disciples experienced doubt because they could not understand.

Amazing. And lovingly understood by the heart of God.

So as I believed for my own healing from cancer, and also during the days I had held on to faith with both hands during my husband's illnesses, the doubt that crept in at times was "distadzo" doubt. I believed God would heal, restore, and keep all His promises to us, but I just did not understand how it would all happen.

Beloved, we need to use the Word of God as a sword. Use it to cut through and clear the way. Clear away doubts, as well as fear, worry, insignificance just as it cleared the fear of doubting out of my mind.

And then go one step further. When an understanding comes from the heart of God to bring you peace, or joy, or freedom—claim it as your own and allow your life and emotions to really be changed by it.

Too often, we receive a breakthrough from God and rejoice in it for that specific trial or for a short season in our life. But then, the next time we come up against another mountain to climb, we forget that amazing thing we learned "back there." I encourage you to hang on to those treasures He gives to you. He will help you now, and next time too! Don't discard them and allow the same pitfalls and fears to rob you of your victory over and over again.

Let freedom build in your life, strengthening and growing as God gives you victory over one situation after another. He wants that for you!

Thoughts to ponder

- What have you been waiting on God for; in your family, your children, your life circumstances, and you wonder if He even cares anymore?
- Ponder times that God has shown His faithfulness to see you through a situation in your life to victory.
- Identify areas of your life where you might have "diakrino" doubt or "distadzo" doubt. Give them both up to God!

Crafted declarations to proclaim:

Lord, I believe Your promises, and I declare that You will give me the strength and courage to follow You through any circumstance that I must face in my life.

I acknowledge You are sovereign, Lord. I will not find my victory in circumstances, but I will find my victory in the Lord Jesus Christ.

Jesus, I will not allow what I have been through in my life to determine what is real. You are real, Jesus. I proclaim my life does not speak louder to me than Your truth.

CHAPTER 9:

A Battle for Destiny ~ 2008

(For the complete story, please read my book titled *A Battle for Destiny* Published 2010. Available on Amazon)

September 12, 2008. A normal Friday morning at the office changed suddenly when my cell phone rang. I smiled as I saw my husband's picture on the caller ID. But as soon as I heard his voice, I knew something was wrong, terribly wrong. Our lives would not be "normal" again for a very long time.

I heard an anguished moan when he said, "I'm throwing up blood!" I knew instantly that what the doctors had been saying was a possibility for the past eighteen years had suddenly happened. I understood all too well what was taking place. Dwight was hemorrhaging from varicose veins in his esophagus, and because he also took blood-thinning medication, I knew he could bleed to death very quickly.

"Where are you?" I said.

"I'm behind a store by my truck!" (He was at work, making a delivery.)

"Is there anyone around?"

"No, I'm all alone. I've called the plant, and they called 911!"

"How far is it to the front of the store?"

"Too far, I can't make it!"

"You have to! Start walking! How far are you now?"

"My arm is going numb!"

"Don't stop! Keep on walking!"

By this time, the women I work with at the headquarters of Aglow International had heard my frantic phone conversation and gathered around the door of my office. They, too, knew what was happening because they had prayed for my husband many times over the years. I made eye contact with them as I paced the floor of my office, struggled to stay focused, and to keep Dwight talking on the phone. I was compelling him with all the strength in me to fight for life!

My co-workers gathered for prayer in the meeting room of our office and began to fight in prayer with me even while I was still on the cell phone with Dwight. The war that would continue raging for the next fifty-five days had begun.

Looking back at that moment, I believe God filled me with a measure of faith-filled determination that I had not had before. Years of hearing great messages and teachings had filled my head with knowledge of what God had spoken to other people. But here I was suddenly facing a life or death situation, and there was no time to wonder what I needed to do. I believed completely that God wanted to heal my husband. I needed to look to God for how to pray His perfect will and for the faith to follow the guidance I knew He would give to me. I began that moment fighting an unseen battle in the spiritual realm. Even though there was a definite medical explanation for what was happening in Dwight's body, somehow, I "knew" in my spirit that I had to become a defender and not a victim.

After what seemed an eternity, Dwight finally told me he had reached the front door of the store. I heard the voice of a woman helping him lie down on the floor. Then I heard sirens, and suddenly a medic was on the phone asking my husband's name, birth date, and to which hospital I wanted them to take him.

My Aglow sisters were in battle mode with me and didn't ask the questions they knew I couldn't answer. They prayed with me before we left the office, and my co-worker, Martha, drove me to the hospital. All the way to the downtown Seattle hospital, we prayed, declared God's Word, and believed.

At times like those, you can feel so powerless. Something was happening that I did not understand, and yet for years had known it could happen. That really "messes with your mind" and ultimately gets to the very foundation of putting it all in God's hands. I knew that I trusted God. I knew that Dwight did too, and with everything in me, I knew it was important to honor the faith that he and I had talked about so many times.

As Martha drove, we prayed out loud at times and just as loudly in our hearts at other times. I prayed that Dwight would live and not die. I prayed for strength and that God would surround Dwight and all the people at the hospital who were tending to him.

Together, we declared that God's healing power would surround him. We declared that we would believe not just what we saw with our eyes but what we knew in our spirits to be true— that God is all-powerful and He died to heal our diseases.

I could feel the grip of fear trying to overtake me. I clearly remembered the night Dwight I had rushed down I-5 to the emergency room at Harborview Trauma Center, fighting fear and praying everything would be all right.

It made me remember every dreadful moment of that terrible night in July 1992 when we rushed to the hospital after receiving the call about our daughter being in that car accident. I knew that God was hearing my prayers, but I also knew He has a time to bring everyone home to heaven. Our daughter lived on this earth for eighteen years and fourteen days. Then her race was finished (2 Timothy 4:7). Why did it take her such a short time to finish her calling on earth? There is that why question again.

Was Dwight's calling on earth finished? I did not feel it was. Please, God, don't let it be so!

As Martha and I proclaimed God's promises and declared what I knew in my spirit was God's ultimate victory for Dwight—I began to feel an emotion, not of myself, begin to take over. I began to feel the fear being replaced by a determination to do real battle in prayer.

When an inner strength like that suddenly floods into your being, you need to recognize that God is giving you a supernatural grace to face the trial you are walking into. People will say to you, "How did you do it? I could never." The truth is, no, you can't handle those life-changing trials on your own without the supernatural grace of God. And God gives you that grace when you need it.

Sure, bad things happen to good people every day, and people do try to live through crisis in their own strength. But those are the people who don't handle their lives well at that point. Fear and hopelessness drive people to anger, bitterness, running away from family, friends, from life itself. Suicide statistics in today's culture are staggering.

I want to live my life like is described in Hebrews 13:5-6: "For God has said, 'I will never fail you. I will never abandon you.' So we can say with confidence, 'The Lord is my helper, so I will have no fear" (NLT).

It was only the day before that we had consulted with a renowned vascular surgeon, Dr. Kai Johannsen, at Swedish Medical Center in Seattle. Dwight had experienced some bleeding issues a month or so before, and the gastroenterologist who treated him felt it was time to consult with a vascular surgeon about the possibility of some type of surgery to correct the internal problems he had dealt with for so many years. He made the appointment for Dwight with the same doctor who told us eighteen years earlier that there was nothing more he could do for him. We hoped that medical advances over the years had changed that.

At that appointment, we had been encouraged to learn that Dr. Johannsen had actually written a paper a few years earlier addressing this type of medical issue. But, we certainly never thought that confidence would be tested the very next day!

When I arrived in the emergency room, Dwight smiled through a blood-caked mustache and beard when he saw me. We looked at each other with eyes of understanding, not needing many words to know exactly what the other was thinking and feeling. So many times over the past eighteen years, we had been forced to talk about the possibility of this type of thing happening. But nothing prepares you for the reality of such a traumatic moment. I knew exactly what was happening and how quickly he could bleed to death.

It was then I had to draw on that supernatural grace I spoke of earlier to bring my emotions under control. Dwight was smiling at me with love and thankfulness; I was there with him. God's strength was with him, and it was with me too. I threw my "bucket" into the well of grace and strength God had for me and found it was deep enough to meet every need.

The first of many units of blood had already been ordered for him, and even before he was moved out of the emergency room into the intensive care unit (ICU), he filled another nausea bag with blood that he could not afford to lose.

I watched in silent horror. "Oh, God!" was my prayer at that moment.

When this happened, Dwight looked at me and said fiercely, "This will not take me out!" Together we allowed our faith to rise and believed God to carry him through this to a victorious end. This was a powerful and positive confession, and it put us in alignment with one another. We were positioning ourselves to rest in the sovereignty of God. That kind of "rest" is every bit as proactive as doing battle with sword and shield!

Our pastor at the time, Dan Hammer, who now serves as the Senior Apostolic Leader of our church, Sonrise Christian Center, and a missionary friend who had just arrived from India, Pastor Matthew Thomas, came to the hospital en route from the airport. They arrived just as Dwight was being wheeled out of the emergency room and followed us up to the ICU floor. The doctors and nurses were working frantically to stabilize Dwight, but they allowed these two godly men to come in and pray for him in the first moments of what would become a very long time in ICU. It was a holy moment as a hush fell in the room, and the Holy Spirit was invited to comfort, to heal, and to sustain life. One of the nurses also laid hands on Dwight and added her prayers to theirs.

The hours that followed are a blur of many units of blood or plasma flowing into Dwight's arm and of bedpans full of the same bright red blood. Even now, as I remember the scene, it is difficult to comprehend.

Amazingly, the nurses allowed me to stay in the room. They saw I remained calm as I immersed myself into what had to be done. I truly don't know how I was able to do that—except that my spirit was resting and believing in God's sovereignty as I fought physically and in prayer for my husband's life.

Dwight was fully conscious, but we didn't talk much. All our attention was given to hanging on to life. When Dwight did talk, he proclaimed determination to never give up and to fight a battle worthy of giving glory to God. When I heard my husband declare such strength in the face of a scene that screamed of sure disaster, and knowing he and I were joined together as one, how could I do less?

Throughout the night, I attended Dwight as the nurses were able to allow me to do so. When I was asked to step out of the room, I paced the hallway and waiting room praying, declaring scripture, and proclaiming God's promises over my husband. At other times when he was able to doze a little, I sat by his bed praying, mostly in my prayer language. In 1 Corinthians 14, verse two, and verse four, we read, "For if you have the ability to speak in tongues you will be talking only to God ...A person who speaks in tongues is strengthened personally" (NLT). I only wanted to speak to God during those night hours, and I surely needed to be strengthened. Praying in tongues was my lifeline connection to my heavenly Father.

It was during one of those early prayers that first night that God brought to my mind what would carry the course of my prayers for all of the days coming.

A few months earlier, we had attended a conference at our church, and each of the attendees received a prophetic prayer that was recorded on tape. These prayers were spoken over each of us by mature Christian leaders who could spiritually discern what God was saying to us. Prophecies like these are not to tell the future or to tell a person what to do. Instead, they are the way God gives encouragement and confirmation to something He has likely already been speaking to that person, quietly in their heart.

I had transcribed the words that both of us received. I had read them over and over, asking God to show us the meaning and how He intended to use them in our lives.

Dwight's word spoke strongly of his destiny. I knew his destiny had not yet been fulfilled! Hour after hour through the night, I reminded God of that fact and demanded that the enemy of his soul, who is Satan, be rendered powerless in his fight to steal the word of Jesus Christ from us.

In John 10:10, the Bible says that Satan came to earth to kill, steal and destroy. So that makes him my enemy because I knew he would try to steal the destiny God had for Dwight. A mighty strength rose up in me, and I knew I had to fight in prayer to protect what was ours from being stolen!

God gave me the power to intercede in prayer through the Holy Spirit that night. I believe God gave me a gift of intercession, and I was able to pray more boldly than I ever had before. I even reminded God that there were still prayers that God needed Dwight to pray on this earth! As I paced around the waiting room throughout that night, speaking loudly to God and pointing my finger in the air for emphasis, I thought, *Where did that come from? Is it okay to talk to God like that?* Yes, it is! God honors the declarations we make to Him in prayer.

About midnight, the decision was made to sedate and intubate Dwight (insert a breathing tube). He had been given nine units of blood during the past twelve hours, and the doctors knew they had to stop the hemorrhaging to save his life. I was relieved that the sedation eased his suffering, but it also made me feel that he was so far away.

Day 2: Between midnight and 7:00 a.m., he did not have any more bleeding episodes. The sun was shining in the windows of his room, and in the light of day, I could see telltale signs of the massive and frequent blood loss of the night before. Dwight was lying quietly, sedated, connected to the breathing machine.

The attending gastroenterologist was so kind as he touched my shoulder and said, "That was pretty rough, wasn't it?" Then the tears I had held back all night came as I allowed myself to be comforted. The doctor gently told me, "Your husband was very sick last night. Some people don't pull out of that kind of situation." I knew it had been very serious, but to hear a doctor admit that made it all too real.

So God had spared his life that night. I asked if putting in the breathing tube had relaxed his system and made the bleeding stop. The doctor said it was more a combination of all the things they had done and were continuing to do; banding the varicose veins in his esophagus that were bleeding, the various medications, and IVs. "And prayer," I added. The doctor agreed, "Yes, and prayer."

In the long hours of waiting, many scriptures gave me comfort. As I read Psalm 27, a divine security settled on the inside of me. A security so real that it gave me the assurance that God was fully in control.

It was as if the words of Psalm 27 (NKJV) became living and so tangible that I actually saw myself running to "hide in His pavilion" (verse five). "He set me high upon a rock" (verse five), and from that vantage point, I could *see His face*. When He told me to "seek His face" (verse eight), with my whole heart, I responded, "Your face, Lord, I will seek." He led me on a smooth path (verse eleven) "because of my enemies." The enemy of our soul, who is Satan, was attacking us with fear and hopelessness, trying to kill Dwight's body and my faith. And I truly "would have lost heart, unless I had believed that I would see the goodness of the Lord in the land of the living" (verse thirteen). He gave me courage to wait upon Him and to be of good courage, and He truly did "strengthen my heart" (verse fourteen).

Countless times in the following weeks—hundreds, at least—I ran to hide and to rest in the shelter that God provided for me. That is the kind of God we serve, radiating power and authority, ready to do battle for us with sword drawn! Always available, He is waiting with open arms to hide us in the shelter of His love. Allowing us to rest because His greatness is taking care of everything.

Day 3: Thirty-six hours later, they removed the breathing tube, which in itself is a painful and frightening experience. I was asked to stand outside his room, and I listened and prayed as I heard the awful sounds through the curtain. I cringed as I heard him gag and cough, and I prayed God would relieve his suffering.

As soon as I could, I went to his side. Dwight seemed fierce in his determination. His first words to me were, "How many times did Paul suffer thirty-nine lashes?"

I wasn't prepared for his question and, great woman of the Word that I am, responded, "Uh, umm, well, I think…"

He interrupted me, "Five times! And how many times did he suffer for the sake of Christ and thanked God for the privilege?"

As I've said before, we both knew this was a battle in the spiritual realm, and it was a real fight for life. If determination alone was required, we felt up for it and determined to glorify God. I hope that statement doesn't sound lofty or super spiritual. Really, a shift into closer alignment seemed to have happened in our hearts, and we recognized that we had received an assignment that we were determined to complete. We both felt rest in our souls but were battling in our spirits.

That day I received an amazing phone call that told me we were not battling alone!

It was Sunday, and my cell phone had often been ringing through the afternoon with friends and family calling to ask about Dwight. When it rang for the "umpteenth" time, I reached to answer without looking to see who was calling. I was totally surprised to hear our friend Augusta Odoteye's voice, calling all the way from Ghana, frantically asking me, "What's wrong! What has happened! Tell me what is going on there!"

Augusta told me that when she was in church that morning, the Lord impressed thoughts of Dwight so strongly on her heart that she ran forward and threw herself on the altar after the service ended, weeping and interceding for Dwight. She had no idea what was happening in Dwight's life but knew, in her spirit, it was a serious matter. So, when I told her what was happening, she knew God had given her a prayer assignment for her friend Dwight. And we both "knew that we knew" God was fully aware of the battle we were in, and we had no doubt that God would see us through.

Day 6: After the initial battle, the next few days were almost peaceful. The bleeding had stopped, his blood pressure was stabilized, and the decision was made to remove Dwight's spleen to lower blood pressure on the varicose veins in his stomach. We finally had time to talk. The surgery was postponed twice, which was a little stressful, but when we learned that the surgeon had been awake all night doing emergency surgeries and that he had postponed so he could be well-rested for Dwight's surgery, we agreed that was a wise decision.

Normally, people don't remain in ICU after they've stabilized, but given Dwight's precarious situation, they did not want to move him from ICU in case he took a sudden turn for the worse. The nurses who had attended Dwight that first night were happy to see him sitting up in bed and chatting comfortably.

During one of those days, while we were waiting for surgery, Dwight's good friend, Scott, was visiting, and he and Dwight were discussing some scriptures. Suddenly, the curtains at the door of the hospital room opened, and a tall young man asked if he could come in. He was the hospital chaplain assigned to ICU. Chaplain Robert, as I came to know him, entered the room, then stopped and looked surprised. He had "felt" the Spirit of God as he stepped into the room and was happy to pull up a chair. The three men began to share easily with each other. I stood at the foot of the bed feeling that it was a special time for them, and I was not surprised when Dwight told Chaplain Robert that he had a word from God for him. Dwight asked if he could pray for him, and it was a special moment. A very comforting friendship began, and Chaplain Robert stopped in each day after that.

Day 11: Finally, the morning of surgery had come. Chaplain Robert came to Dwight's room to pray with us. It was a sweet and peaceful time. We knew the risks of the surgery but also knew what God had promised. I felt like both of us were marching together into a battle, and I felt faith rise up in me that we would win.

I was told the surgery to remove Dwight's spleen would take three to six hours, then another one to two hours in the recovery room. I settled myself into the family surgical waiting room and made some phone calls to let our family and friends know the surgery was beginning. We surely wanted full prayer coverage at that time! I knew that the loved ones I called would each call many others—so the chain of prayer would be strong and long!

I received a message from the operating room after about two hours telling me the first part of the surgery had gone well, and they were then beginning the splenectomy. The surgeon came out and talked with me about two hours later. The whole thing had taken only four hours. That seemed to be a good sign!

The doctor said the surgery went well, although he was not able to do all that he had hoped. He explained everything he did, even drawing for me a picture of strange shapes and lines to explain why he had made the decisions he did during the surgery. He explained how he had hoped to accomplish a better solution for Dwight's long-term health but that doing any more would have put too great a strain on Dwight's system. During surgery, they gave him several units of blood and also re-circulated 600 cubic centimeters of his own blood back into his system. The removal of Dwight's spleen would significantly reduce the blood pressure in his stomach, but it was not possible to insert a shunt which would have reduced the blood pressure in his esophagus. The doctor said he should be intubated (on the breathing machine) until the next day and out of the hospital in three days, "or until we're comfortable with him going home."

Again, I felt calm and even confident that everything was under control. Now I sometimes wonder about that. Was I really "out of touch" with my emotions? No, I don't think so. I felt so confident in God and in what He had already spoken to my heart that I was able to honestly rest in that knowledge. The Jesus I know cares for me and for my husband so lovingly. He was allowing me to hide, to rest, in His pavilion of faith where panic and worry had no place. He took it all when He died on the cross for me and for you.

Are you going through something in your life so overwhelming that you feel out of touch with your emotions about it? Something that has created such fear and confusion in your life that it has caused you to just shut down and feel numb? Dear one, you can find a place of safety and rest too. Jesus loves you every bit as much as He loves me.

> Ask, and it will be given to you; seek, and you will find; knock, and it will be opened to you. For everyone who asks receives, and he who seeks finds, and to him who knocks it will be opened.
>
> Matthew 7:7-8 (NKJV)

The "you" in this verse means you! And "everyone" means everyone! Jesus has promised this to you.

Day 12: Looking back on this day, I think God had me in a little cocoon, as it was really "the calm before the storm." I had even gone home to sleep the night after his surgery. He had a breathing tube inserted into his mouth and a nose tube to drain fluid out of his stomach. He was receiving large amounts of fluids through IV to keep his blood pressure up and was heavily sedated, yet the doctors seemed pleased with his progress. His eyes were closed, but he would nod when I spoke to him.

As I sat in his room reading, the anesthesiologist stopped by the room to see how his patient was doing. In our brief conversation, I mentioned that Dwight was a very strong and determined man. The doctor's response was amazing.

He said, "Oh, I know he is determined! I could tell even by how his internal organs looked and how his body responded during surgery."

He knew Dwight was determined from his internal organs! There were a million questions I wanted to ask about that but was unable to take the doctor's time with them. We might think that if we talk bravely or show courage or determination by our body language, we will be a determined person. Like we can "will" ourselves to be determined.

But even determination is a gift from God, imparted to the inside of us. It is a gift like other gifts that Jesus offers to us, as stated in 1 Corinthians 12; words of wisdom, words of knowledge, faith, gifts of healings, working of miracles, prophecy, discerning of spirits, different kinds of tongues, the interpretation of tongues. We can take those gifts and make them part of ourselves, or we can reject them, choosing to live in our own feebleness. Let us embrace every one of the gifts God offers to us.

"But one and the same Spirit works all these things, distributing to each one individually as He wills" (1 Corinthians 12:11, NKJV).

As that first day after surgery wore on, the doctor's concern for Dwight's condition grew. He had lost a lot of blood during surgery, and his body was severely stressed even though the full surgery had not been accomplished. Now it was taking him longer than normal to make the initial recovery from surgery. His diaphragm had to be pushed up to remove the spleen, so his lung was partially deflated. The breathing machine was necessary to bring his lung back to capacity. I counted fourteen IV medications, all running fluids into his body to keep him alive, plus the breathing machine.

By this time, they knew this would not be a routine surgical recovery. They moved Dwight to another room on the surgical ICU floor, closer to the nurses' station.

The room was large with a long, padded window seat. I wanted to stay close, so I had a pillow and blanket, intending to rest my body on that window seat through the night, even as I sought a place of rest for my spirit. I was having flashbacks to 1988 when I had spent many nights in a recliner by Dwight's hospital bed, wondering how long until he would recover.

I was grateful that I was allowed to stay in the ICU room with Dwight. Very late that night, as the nurse and I were standing on either side of his bed, I was increasingly concerned because his condition seemed to be worsening. But I also knew it was that difficult post-surgery time. I was still hanging on to what the doctor had told me the day before, that Dwight would be able to go home in just a few days. However, what my eyes saw was making me feel afraid. "Oh, God," I prayed. "Help me walk by faith and not by sight" (2 Corinthians 5:7, NKJV).

The ICU nurse was efficiently and quietly checking all the IVs and tubes when suddenly the tube through his nose to his stomach turned red. Neither of us said anything. We both knew what was happening. He was bleeding again. I stepped out of the way and retreated to my window seat as the room became a beehive of activity. The medical team quickly assembled and began immediately to do what they could to turn this situation around. They took Dwight off the blood-thinning medication. He needed it to keep his blood from clotting, but it was also working against him, causing him to bleed in his stomach.

From that window seat, I watched and prayed. My silent prayers weren't so eloquent. They were more like, "Oh, God, please help us!" I was thankful that the nurses let me sit there in the room, and I kept myself from asking questions so they could stay focused on doing all they could to keep my husband alive.

I remember feeling a "controlled panic;" if there is such a thing. I reminded God of His promises. I was doing all I knew to do. "God! We're in trouble down here!" I called "the troops" for prayer. Over the next several hours, I watched and prayed as the bleeding slowed and then stopped.

The surgeon checked on Dwight even through the night hours. He told me that the bleeding was "worrisome." He told me something like, "We'll do our best to get him through this." I asked if he had a concern that he wouldn't be able to do that. He told me that my husband had been very sick but had been getting better since the surgery. "Let's hope we can get him over this crisis tonight and that he'll keep on improving. Dwight is a very unusual case."

I felt as though I was hovering somewhere between nightmare and reality. I had no doubt that Jesus was with us and no question about God's love. I could find rest in that. But sometimes, the unthinkable *does* happen, and I knew that all too well. I prayed God would not send those angels to escort him to heaven that night.

By morning he had stabilized. The bleeding had stopped; he was fully sedated but still on the ventilator.

I went home that night to sleep and had a dream about Dwight. In my dream, I was at the hospital, it seemed like I was in a corridor by the cafeteria, and Dwight suddenly came walking around the corner. He was a little unsteady on his feet but was fully dressed. He wore his work clothes—jeans, a navy blue shirt, and suspenders. But I immediately noticed something unusual. He had sawdust on his right collar.

The next day Chaplain Robert came to see Dwight, and I told him about this dream. He said, "Jesus was a carpenter. Dwight has been close enough to Jesus that he got sawdust on his collar."

Day 16: Several days passed, and Dwight's condition remained stable. He was still alive.

The nurse told me that through the night, Dwight had eliminated six liters of fluid—about one and a half gallons! His body was certainly being put through the paces. They wanted to get him off the breathing tube and did another breathing trial in the morning. He breathed strongly enough on his own but had a lot of trouble waking up. At 3:00 p.m., the decision was made to remove the breathing tube. I had wanted this very badly as it was so difficult to see Dwight struggling so to breathe, but when the tube was removed, and he couldn't seem to wake up, it was another great concern to me and also to the nurse caring for him.

When you're in the hospital for a long time with a loved one, you yearn for anything normal. You wonder if life will ever be normal again, so you are eager to grasp anything that feels like life as you once knew it. Our grandson, Christopher, eight years old at the time, loved to be at our home and spent every weekend with us. It had been hard for him to know Grandpa was very sick and in the hospital and to not stay overnight at our house as usual. This was a Saturday night, so I decided to go home for the night (and take a shower and wash my hair), pick up Christopher to stay overnight and bring him to church as usual, and then go to the hospital to see his grandpa. Dwight would surely be awake by then, and we would have a nice visit—almost like normal.

Christopher was happy to be at our house, and even though Grandpa wasn't there, we would get to see him tomorrow. He was already in bed when, about 9:00 p.m., I called the hospital to check on Dwight. The nurse who answered the phone in ICU said that Dwight's nurse was in his room and couldn't come to the phone and to please call back later.

I called again in a bit and was told the same thing. Then I knew something was not right. Finally, a third time I called, the doctor came on the line and told me Dwight was bleeding again, probably from both his esophagus and his stomach. They had to re-insert the breathing tube. The doctor told me, "His options are not very good. It doesn't look good for him."

I phoned my daughter, Terry, and told her I was bringing Christopher home and she needed to quickly arrange care for him and come to the hospital with me. En route to the hospital, we made urgent phone calls to all the family who lived in the area—Dwight's sister, two of his brothers, his mom, and our pastor. We didn't know what to tell them, except that Dwight was in great distress, and we needed them to pray! Terry and I didn't speak much as we sped down the interstate highway through Seattle toward the hospital. All we could do was utter short prayers shot heavenward like flaming arrows sent up to alert our heavenly allies that we needed help. Those prayers all seemed to begin with, "Oh, God!"

Terry and I arrived at the hospital at about 10:30 p.m. When we reached Dwight's room, there were five or six doctors and internists in the hallway outside of his room, all discussing his case. I later asked the nurse why all those doctors were there, and he said whenever there is a traumatic case like this, the word is spread, and all the specialists on duty come to be ready if they are needed. I was grateful to every one of them.

One of the nurses spoke to me before I went into Dwight's room. She asked how I was holding up. She said she had lost her mother recently and understood the roller coaster of emotions. I looked at her, grateful for the human connection, but also unable—or maybe unwilling is a better word—to give myself into that place of sympathetic concern. I told her I was doing fine and was in a mode of intense focus. I think I said I felt "all business" at the moment. She said she understood. I'm sure they see every emotion and response imaginable in ICU!

What I meant was, I felt I couldn't spend time right then for my own tears and sympathy. I felt an intensity that demanded my full attention to the battle we were in. I believe this was the first moment that I realized the full scope of this war. It was an intensity demanding all my focus and strength, as when a woman is about to give birth. Nothing else matters except what she needs to do to bring forth that baby. That night, nothing else mattered except what we needed to do to fight and win this fierce skirmish. There was no doubt that this was a spiritual battle!

To "fight" in prayer might seem like two concepts that do not go together. Many of us were raised in Sunday school learning sweet prayers asking Jesus to bless the little children and to gently lead us. But we must also know Jesus as He is described in Revelation 19:11-16. Jesus Christ, riding out of heaven on a white horse, making war on the enemy, Satan. Read those powerful verses and be filled with courage as you picture Jesus coming to fight for you!

We went into Dwight's room, and although they had cleaned it, we could clearly see the remnants of what had been a traumatic event. I was told that at about 9:00 p.m., the nurse was right beside Dwight's bed, with the head of the bed inclined so he could breathe more easily, when suddenly he coughed a little and then violently vomited what seemed to be a huge amount of blood. The nurse, who had been a medic in Iraq during Desert Storm, said, "It looked like a war zone in here." I think the Lord blinded my eyes to this, but my brother-in-law told me later that he noticed bloody fingerprints on the monitors by Dwight's hospital bed.

By 11:00 p.m., family members and several prayer warriors from church had gathered for what became an all-night prayer vigil. Pastor Dan had called our friend Bob, who rallied the troops and gathered several men to come to the hospital. All of these dear ones—family and friends—dropped everything and came in the middle of the night to fight with and for us. Amazing! We surrounded Dwight's bed and prayed, stormed heaven, declared and proclaimed. We did all we knew to do. Jesus of Revelation 19 was in our midst to battle with us.

One of the men from our church, Todd, encouraged me to lead in these prayers and proclamations. At first, I felt timid to do this while surrounded by these mighty men of God. But then he reminded me that, as Dwight's wife, we are joined together as one, so my prayers had the utmost authority in that setting. I pushed aside the feelings of timidity and stepped into the authority that I then, perhaps for the first time, really understood was mine.

When the nurses came in to care for Dwight, we moved to the waiting room, just two doors down the hallway. We filled that small room and continued our vigil there until we could go back into his room again to pray. God had said Dwight had a destiny that was not yet fulfilled! I knew I needed to continue to pray in my newfound authority. That gave me courage to remind God of His promise and to proclaim that it comes to pass.

I was anointed that night with power and determination from the Holy Spirit as I read out loud the psalms God had given to me for Dwight. I read them over his body, inserting his name as I read, as proclamations of who God was to Dwight while the others laid hands on my husband, surrounding his bed and agreeing with my prayers.

> In You, O Lord, I put my trust;
> …Incline Your ear to me, and save me.
> Be my strong refuge,
> …For You are my hope, O Lord God;
> …But I will hope continually,
> And will praise You yet more and more.
> …You, who have shown me great and severe troubles,
> Shall revive me again.
>
> Psalm 71 (NKJV)

> The Lord is my light and salvation;
> Whom shall I fear?
> The Lord is the strength of my life;
> Of whom shall I be afraid?
> …For in the time of trouble
> He shall hide me in His pavilion;
> … He shall set me high upon a rock.
>
> Psalm 27:1, 5 (NKJV)

I read and proclaimed again that prophetic word Dwight had received some months before that spoke clearly of his destiny.

By 7:00 a.m., some of the group needed to leave, but we all felt we had accomplished what had been necessary that night. Dwight was still alive. God was in control.

I deeply appreciated the attitudes of the nurses on duty that night and how they allowed us to spend time around Dwight's bed. We, of course, stepped aside whenever they needed to care for Dwight, but they allowed us the freedom to do what we needed to do also. I believe they recognized that we were not a bunch of "religious fanatics" performing strange practices. I believe they saw we were mature Christians with a purpose. Often, in settings like hospitals, people are afraid to demonstrate their faith, worried about what others might think. After that night, not a single doctor or nurse commented negatively to me about what they witnessed from me or the many dear men and women who came to pray for Dwight. We had earned authority, and we were walking in it.

Day 22: It had been nearly a week since the last episode. He was still intubated and unable to communicate with me. At this point, Dwight's condition surely didn't look good, but the doctors assured me he was doing well and it would get better. I hung on to their words and to God's promises because what my eyes saw was very different.

It is at times like these—when what we see and hear do not match what we know God has spoken to us—that we must see and hear through the Holy Spirit. I knew it was wisdom to follow the doctor's skilled instructions and to allow all the medicines and procedures, but I also knew that what God had spoken was every bit as real. I thanked God for the skill of the doctors and nurses, for the medicines God had created for our use, and even for the machines and procedures used to carry those medicines into Dwight's body. But they were not the source of healing. God, in all His power and glory, was our source every moment of every day. I sat on that window seat in Dwight's room, resting, believing in God's greatness.

It had been six days since Dwight had gone through that latest bleeding episode. The doctors had again greatly increased his IV fluid intake. It was necessary to fill his body with fluid in order to keep his blood pressure up but also to try and control the bleeding risk in his abdomen and esophagus. I didn't understand all of that, but what I did know was that Dwight's body now became so full of fluid I wondered how his skin could stretch enough to contain it.

He was partially sedated and on the ventilator. His legs were as hard and round as tree trunks, and fluid "leaked" from his hands and arms at sites where IV needles had previously pierced his skin. The nurses kept towels under his arms that became soaked with the fluid his body could not contain. It had been nearly a month since he had eaten any food, but now he weighed eighty pounds more than when he was first admitted to the hospital. Eighty pounds of extra fluid in his body. It seemed impossible.

I have great respect for the nurses that care for patients in ICU. The doctors write the orders, but it is the nurses who carry out the plan, and Dwight's "plan" was changing daily. The nurses, both male and female, all treated Dwight with great respect. I had brought a photo to display on the shelf of his room that showed the vigorous and healthy man that Dwight really is. The photo was taken on Puget Sound on our little fishing boat and showed Dwight and our grandson Christopher, both in their matching leather cowboy hats, smiling at each other with all the confidence and happiness of a man and his grandson out fishing. I wanted people to know who Dwight really was, not just the man lying helpless in that bed. I wanted them to see a man who loved life and loved his family.

Dwight and Christopher

Day 27: October 8, 2008, our grandson Christopher's ninth birthday, but there would be no birthday party for him at the hospital as I had hoped. The ventilator tube had been removed, but Dwight was not recovering from the sedation. I had great expectations that Dwight would wake up today. I missed my husband!

By the evening, he was able to keep his eyes open and was trying to come out of the thick fog that held his brain captive. As

I held his hand, I asked him to squeeze my fingers. No movement at all. I gently asked him again to squeeze my hand. He couldn't do it, and tears began to roll down his cheeks as he looked at me with no other emotion on his face. So we just sat there crying together. I had no way of knowing what he was thinking, but I was wondering what our lives would be like in the future or if there would be a future. Would he ever be "himself" again? Would he be able to talk, laugh, and communicate? Would he ever work again or do any of the things he loves to do?

Day 30: What had begun as a day of hopeful progress ended far differently. Throughout the day, the doctors were encouraged and positive about Dwight's progress. Physical therapists even worked with him a little. Although the sedation was still affecting him and he acted frustrated, I felt comfortable enough to go home that evening to shower and sleep in my own bed.

On the way home, I had a flat tire on the freeway! That had never happened to me before. My first thought was to call Dwight. He would know exactly what I should do. But I had to handle this myself. If I had been home in my driveway, I would have figured out how to change it myself, but here on the freeway, with cars speeding by, it seemed too dangerous. So I took advantage of our seldom-used roadside assistance. I was so grateful when I finally arrived home driving on my spare tire!

Before going to sleep, I phoned the hospital and learned Dwight's breathing had become labored. I dressed quickly and, driving our other car, returned to the hospital, arriving about 11:00 p.m. (an hour's drive at that time of night.) When I reached his room, it was filled with people. The respiratory doctors had brought in the ventilator that seemed to fill the room and were preparing to re-intubate Dwight. His nurse was there, of course, as well as other nurses on duty that night that had cared for him at others times. They had gathered when they heard the news that he was being re-intubated for the fourth time and were concerned. He had been off the ventilator for only twenty-seven hours. Dwight was known throughout the floor as a man with great determination and strength, and they all felt so bad to see him go through this again.

When I reached the room, the head of Dwight's bed was inclined to help him breathe. His face was red from struggling for air, his whole body shaking as he fought for each breath. The numbers on his monitor were too high for me to comprehend. His nurse told me not to look at them.

Even as all the hospital personnel stood by, I put my face to Dwight's ear and, through my tears, proclaimed what I knew we both believed. "Determination, hang on, never give up! God is in control! He is our safe refuge! I love you!"

I wept as the ventilator tube was inserted. This time they didn't even make me leave the room, but I couldn't bear to watch. It brought life-giving oxygen but also took my husband away to a place where I couldn't reach him. I wondered how long it would be this time.

The next morning, the doctor explained it was not actually a huge setback. However, it sure felt huge to me! He explained Dwight still had too much fluid in his body, and his lungs were like sponges, so he couldn't breathe. It would just take more time.

Time. More time.

Now when I think back to those days, even I wonder how I spent my time day after day. Of course, I wished I could spend my days anywhere else except that hospital. Every couple of days, I would take a walk outside and often would browse through the gift shop off the main lobby of the hospital on my way back upstairs. One day I realized the clerks in the gift shop were talking about me. "She's still here," I heard one of them say in hushed tones. *Yup*, I thought. *I'm still here.* And every day, I wondered how much longer it would be before *we* could go home.

⁎

I'm not a naïve person, and I know that people do lose their loved ones to death—every day. Incredibly one Sunday afternoon, while our friends Scott and Kay were with me in the hospital room, Kay received a phone call. Her mother had suddenly died in Redding, California. She had spoken with her just a few hours before as they arrived at church that morning. We both wept as we held on to each other in disbelief, praying for God's merciful presence to surround us.

I am aware, even as I tell my story, there will be someone who will read this and think, *I've been through tough times too. I know exactly what that experience is like. My situation was even worse than hers. I believed as strongly as she did, and I battled for healing too. But my loved one did die! Why?*

Dear one, I don't know why. As I wrote in chapter seven, when my daughter died, I asked that question a million times. "God, if You will just tell me why, I'll understand, and then I'll find peace." But He never answered that question. Instead, a few years after our daughter died, He spoke something to my heart one day when I had—again—been crying out to God and asking Him, "How long will I have to feel this pain? Just tell me why!" Suddenly, He spoke to my heart, "As long as it takes. I am in control, and I will walk with you."

"As long as it takes? What does that mean?" Well, He didn't answer that question either. But I've come to know that can mean a very long time.

Walking through any kind of long-term trial or painful situation isn't easy. It's hard, gut-wrenching, a battle every step of the way. But I've learned something through the times of trial I've walked through. I've learned that God does stay close—"for as long as it takes" for me to truly come to that place of rest with Him. He laughs with me. He cries with me. He lives my pain with me because He has felt it too.

But as I told you before about what I had read in that Philip Yancey book—through it all, He asks, "Do you love Me. Do you love Me even now? Will you trust My love, even through this?"

And that propels me back to Psalm 27:8 (NKJV) "When you said, 'Seek My face,' my heart said to You, 'Your face, Lord, I will seek.'" Yes, Lord, I do love You! I run to hide in the high tower You have prepared for me. I find my rest in You—the only kind of rest that is truly real.

Day 36: ICU psychosis—another new term I learned about. Dwight was awake (at least he appeared to be awake), and he could breathe on his own. He was trying to communicate but, whenever he spoke, his words came out in a jumbled rush of sounds that were impossible to decipher.

A doctor explained this phenomenon of ICU psychosis to me. He explained that in intensive care units, there is twenty-four-hour activity because patients need that constant 24/7 care. There is little or no difference in the activity levels between night and day. I could well understand that because I had been living in that environment myself for over a month!

But, while I could find relief in taking a short walk outside or wearing night shades and earplugs and sleeping on my cot in the back corner of his ICU room through some of the middle-of-the-night poking and prodding, Dwight as the patient could not. And even when he was sedated, he was not in a state of rest. So part of ICU psychosis is actually being sleep-deprived!

This went on for days. Sometimes, the nurse or I would hear a word we could understand, and we would try to respond appropriately. I was careful to try not to guess too fast because Dwight would roll his eyes and just look away. He knew what he was trying to say!

But once in the midst of a string of garbled sounds, I heard him say the word "chair." So the physical therapy nurse agreed to sit him up on the edge of the bed for the first time. He was able to sit up for about four minutes, with three people holding him upright. He didn't have the strength to hold his head up, but I bent way down to look up at his face and saw a tiny smile come to his lips as he sat there. Even small victories are important!

That one tiny smile was remarkable because, for days, there was no emotion in his face, delayed reaction, and extreme weakness. All this was part of the ICU psychosis. I was surprised one day to realize his sense of humor was intact. I asked if he could hear me, and he shook his head, no! But all with no emotion in his eyes or his face. It made me laugh.

Another time, Chaplain Robert had stopped by for his afternoon visit. The head of Dwight's bed was raised a little, and the chaplain and I were each sitting in chairs on either side of the bed. There were lots of pillows in the bed, under his arms and legs to keep them cushioned against bed sores. We were chatting quietly, not knowing if Dwight was hearing or registering at all with our conversation. Suddenly, we saw Dwight make an awful grimace as if in great pain! No sound came from his wide-open mouth, but we could instantly see he was in anguish. We both jumped and then realized Chaplain Robert had been leaning on Dwight's leg with his elbow—and it hurt! Chaplain Robert felt awful about it, but at the same time, we had to laugh. Dwight couldn't speak, but he could certainly communicate!

I knew my husband was still "in there," but how could he get out and be himself again? O God—You are my strong tower. I run to find safety in You. You are my rest, O Lord.

Day 39: It was getting so hard to wait, day after day, for some glimmer of progress. I almost said, "glimmer of hope," but thankfully, I always did have hope. I don't understand how that could be, except that God was there with me, walking through each day with me. He did that because I had invited Him to be there. God was my strength, and in that, I had the strength I needed to wait. It was all part of resting in God.

> I love you, Lord; you are my strength.
>
> The Lord is my rock, my fortress, and my savior; my God is my rock, in whom I find protection. He is my shield, the power that saves me, and my place of safety.
>
> I called on the Lord, who is worthy of praise, and he saved me from my enemies.
>
> Psalm 18:1-3 (NLT)

Do you know that you have control over where your emotions go or where your emotions can take you? When circumstances threaten to push you emotionally "over the edge," you can choose to take control over them. You find the strength to do that when you look to God, who loves you with all of His strength.

In Psalm 91:14, "The Lord says, 'I will rescue those who love me. I will protect those who trust in my name'" (NLT).

Finally, little by little, in very small ways, I watched Dwight begin to respond. It was amazing to me, and I rejoiced at every tiny victory. I witnessed his determination and did all I could to help him.

He reached out for my hands then worked hard for a few seconds to pull himself up. He looked at his fingernails after I commented they were getting long and needed to be trimmed. He scratched his chin, and he pulled his blankets up with both hands.

These were amazing victories. He was slowly beginning to fight his way back.

Day 40: Dwight was still very sick. This evening he had pain, and he couldn't talk. I was standing by his bed just looking into his face, and the nurse, Melanie, was on the other side of his bed doing something with his IV lines. The room was dimly lit and felt peaceful.

As we stood there, the nurse and I both watched as Dwight reached up and touched my face. Then he raised his hand and looked up as if he was looking at something far past the ceiling. He just stayed like that, with his hand raised and looking up to the ceiling for a minute or so. The nurse looked at me with a question in her eyes.

Finally, I whispered into his ear, "You can't go. You have to stay here. You still have things to do here." Slowly, he lowered his arm and closed his eyes.

Day 43: Today, I was told that Dwight is now out of the first critical stage of needing life support and into the second stage of rehabilitation. I felt happy to hear this, of course—for them to be talking about rehab, he must truly be getting better. But the man I saw lying in that bed surely was a long way from being able to do the required three hours of physical therapy per day!

It was October 24, forty-three days since Dwight had entered the hospital. And for the majority of those days, he was heavily sedated and could not move his muscles at all. Dwight's body had been severely bloated with fluid for so long, masking the muscle loss that was occurring each day. Now, with the fluid retention reversed, his arms and legs were literally skin on bone, with no muscle tone whatsoever. It seemed the muscles were not even there anymore! Today he was given the okay to eat soft food, but he could not hold a spoon in his hand; he could barely lift his own arm or adjust himself in the bed. My once strong and robust husband was very nearly helpless.

But I want to encourage anyone who may be facing physical therapy rehab or loved ones who have watched as once-strong bodies are reduced to skin and bone. In your natural mind, you wonder how they can ever become strong again. How can their bodies ever regain their former shape and vigor? I can testify that this is possible!

As the physical therapy technicians came two times each day, they slowly and carefully helped Dwight to move his body and to strain his muscles to begin working again. I was told that "muscles have memory," and when they are forced to begin moving again, they will also begin to grow and strengthen. This is exactly what happened in Dwight's body.

At first, it took two technicians and me to hold him upright to sit on the side of the bed. Now they were working with him each day to try and stand to his feet. It took several days for his legs to find their strength, but finally, with a technician on each side of him and a lifting belt around his waist, Dwight stood to his feet. We all cheered, and he looked at me with a tired smile. I gave him a hug as we stood face to face for the first time in so many days. He told me he wanted to go home tomorrow!

Day 48: Today's blood tests showed high ammonia levels, explaining the confusion, but also very low blood levels. Seven units of blood were quickly ordered, four platelets and three red. They brought a respirator to the hallway just outside Dwight's hospital room and had a Brighton balloon catheter ready "just in case." They had already used this dangerous but necessary "internal tourniquet" once before to stop bleeding in his esophagus. Even the nurses, who had seen countless critical events, expressed concern for what was happening.

Dwight spoke little. He prayed, "God help me." And he said he felt he had nothing left. I made some phone calls to again "alert the troops." Bob went to church and rallied everyone in all the Wednesday night classes to pray for Dwight. One of the pastors called and talked to me on the phone, and our friends Scott and Kay came to the hospital and played worship music through the night hours. We all felt the "full-on" attack, and our response in God was swift.

Day 50: A line from today's entry in the devotional I was reading stayed with me all day. "If the storm comes and I know I am in the will of God, then little else matters." We knew the storm was raging around us. We also knew God was with us.

As I said earlier, I had kept notes each day because I felt, someday, Dwight might want to know about everything that had happened to him. At this point in my writing and going through all those notes, I honestly thought, *My God, is this ever going to end?* I knew I had lived it, but as I was re-telling the story, it seemed almost bizarre that there was such an onslaught day after day after day.

But I was soon to find out that the enemy of our souls was finally weighing his options and realizing he was *not* going to win this battle after all! Things were about to change!

Day 51: November 1—Victory!

Very early this morning, Dwight called to me from where I was sleeping in my roll-away bed in the corner. It had been a very fitful night. But now, as he spoke to me, there was a new clarity that he had not had before. He was so confused about where he was, what was happening, why no one was around, and no one was helping us. I sat by his bed and explained what I could about everything that had taken place during the past fifty days. I told him about all the wonderful doctors and nurses who were helping us, the surgeries, and the many blood transfusions. He listened, amazed, with tears running down his face. He asked questions, and we talked a long time in those early morning hours.

Then we both dozed a little, me with my head resting on the side of his bed. When we woke up, he was back! I was amazed! The fog and confusion had lifted, and he was Dwight again. I said, "I missed you." He said, "I missed you, too."

During the night, he had been in a battle in his mind with hopelessness trying to overtake him. When we talked about it later, it seemed to us like one last swipe of the enemy to try to make him give up. It didn't work, and the attack came to an end. It makes me remember what Kathy, one of my co-workers at Aglow, had told me—the enemy's power is so limited, and at some point, he will know he has lost the battle. Well, he has lost, and Jesus Christ is the victor in Dwight's life! Glory to God.

Dwight was still very weak and working hard with physical therapists to be strong enough to leave the hospital and enter rehab. He was gaining strength daily. I watched him pick up a carton of milk from the table in front of him and bring it to his lips to drink it, and I thanked God. He could not yet stand or walk unaided but was getting better each day.

Day 55: November 5, 2008.

Fifty-five days had passed since September 12, when Dwight was first admitted to ICU. Now it was November 5, just four days after he had really woken up and become fully conscious of his situation and his surroundings.

Today, Dwight was transferred out of ICU at Swedish Medical Center in Seattle to Providence Hospital rehab in Everett. I left my window seat, my place of restful warring in the spirit. It had served me well.

Dwight worked hard in rehab and came home in just ten days, much sooner than expected. He could no longer work, so he became medically retired and found new ways to fill his days. I went back to my full-time work at the Aglow office. Life resumed, and again, we again found our "new normal."

That new normal included time for Dwight to go on some mission trips. From 2010 through 2015, he was happy to have the opportunity to travel on mission trips to Zimbabwe, Thailand, the Philippines, Korea, and Japan. God was using him strongly in discernment and deliverance prayer. How he loved to pray with people and see God heal and set them free!

It was only a few months after Dwight came home from the hospital when, in March 2009, my mother came to live with us. My dad had died seven years before, and my only sister had serious health problems. So, when my dear mom reached the time in her life when she needed daily help, we suggested she move from Minnesota to live with us in Washington. With Dwight home, he could provide the care she needed during the day, and I could see to her needs when I was home from work. She finally agreed to move to Washington when we promised that we would bring her back to Minnesota when Jesus called her home to heaven, to be buried next to my dad. And three years later, in March 2012, we did just that.

Those three years with my mom were precious, and I was able to help her grieve the loss of her own daughter. My sister, Susan, died in September 2009 following a long illness. This was a huge loss for her family and all of us.

Dearly loved family members can never be replaced, but God delights in giving us new joys to help fill those holes left in our lives.

Shortly after returning to Washington after my sisters' funeral, Mom and I went to an Aglow meeting in our community. I knew a couple of the women there, but my mom knew no one. So, I was surprised to look across the room during the fellowship time and see her visiting with a young woman I had never seen before. They were laughing and talking as though they were old friends. I soon learned Mary and my mom were destined to be God's gifts to each other.

Mary Pederson's sweet Norwegian mother had died a few years earlier, and Mary missed her. She asked God to help her meet an older Norwegian lady with who she could enjoy friendship to fill that empty spot in her heart. It was shortly after praying that request to God that she met my mom. It was a friendship made in heaven for sure.

Mary and my mom "adopted" each other, so God had given me a sister as well. My birth sister Susan never met Mary, but I know they would have loved each other. Ever since then, and forevermore, our hearts are joined as family.

God's love knows just what we need, and He goes before each of us to fill our lives with more of Himself.

Thoughts to ponder

- What frightens you the most about times of waiting on God?
- Do you believe God is in the waiting?
- What is your understanding of "supernatural grace"?

CHAPTER 10:

Declaration—I Want to Live! ~ 2018

Ten years later—September 21, 2018—another team of doctors stood around Dwight's bed in the ER of the Veterans Hospital in Seattle, all with somber looks on their faces.

Tests had confirmed aggressive lymphoma cancer throughout his chest cavity and abdomen, and it had metastasized to his lungs, liver, stomach, and colon. The head doctor looked at Dwight and said, "Mr. Brooks, what would you like us to do for you?"

At that moment, I knew they were fully prepared to hear Dwight tell them to just make him comfortable for however many days he had left to live. I held my breath waiting for his response. But that was not what God was speaking to his spirit. Instead, he declared strongly to the doctors, "I want to live!"

I exhaled and thanked God for this response. I knew the decision had to be his, and I knew my husband and his strong will to live, so I was not surprised. However, I could tell the doctors were taken aback, but to their credit, they immediately said, "Okay, we will do all we can to get you through this."

And so, the next journey began.

It had been a busy summer, and we had not taken any vacation time. We decided to do something very different (for us), so Dwight researched the internet and rented a condo on the Oregon coast for a week in late September.

We drove to the beautiful Oregon coast excited for a week away, filled with new experiences and no responsibilities. We had packed a cooler full of food to make our own meals in the mini-kitchen of the condo and looked forward to walking the beaches and exploring the thrift shops along with the little coastal villages in that area. We love times like that.

In recent months Dwight hadn't been feeling well, but all the symptoms he was having were easy to explain away for logical reasons. He had been diagnosed as pre-diabetic, so he was trying to lose weight and happy that weight was coming off pretty quickly. In addition, there was a growing pain in his abdomen in the area of his past surgery, now some years ago. Things change as we get older, right?

But now, as the week progressed, Dwight felt worse each day. He had some alarming attacks of pain but did not want to "give in" to them and spoil our vacation. Each day we did a little sightseeing and then rested in the condo, sitting on the deck looking out onto the Pacific Ocean reading or watching TV. By Thursday, he could no longer manage, and when his body began to shake uncontrollably, we knew I had to take him to the emergency room of the small local hospital in the town where we were staying. Pain meds were given. Tests were run. We wondered if he had some kind of severe indigestion or had eaten something that had made him sick. I thought he might need to drink some Sprite to make him feel better.

When the doctor, a pretty young woman who was a physician's assistant, came into the ER examination room, she carried a box of tissues, and I could tell she had been crying herself. We were completely unprepared for what she had to tell us. The CAT scan showed cancer throughout Dwight's abdomen.

What? Just yesterday, we were having fun watching whales from shore on the Oregon coast! Now you tell us he has cancer? That had not been on our radar in any way! Our minds reeled as we made a couple of phone calls to our daughter and to some good friends who would begin to intercede for us and talked with the ER staff to figure out what to do.

They called the nearest VA hospital in Portland, but they had no bed space available. We knew we wanted to get closer to home and, because Dwight was already connected with the doctors at the VA in Seattle, we were quite sure we could be seen there.

It was decided they would keep Dwight overnight at the hospital to manage his pain. I drove back to the condo alone and packed up all our things, and tried to get some rest. My prayers were fluctuating between great faith, remembering how God had worked in our lives in the past, and fear that took my breath away. How many more times would God bring Dwight from the threshold of death's door? We all would die someday. Was this going to be Dwight's last battle?

Everything in me was ready to fight again for my husband's life. I was not ready to let him go! "God, please touch him. God, please sustain his life and give us more years together. Jesus, please give me the strength to go through whatever is facing us this time."

The next morning, I arrived at the hospital about 7:30 a.m. with the car packed and filled with gas for our four-hour drive back to Seattle. Dwight had been kept sedated overnight because of the severe pain he was experiencing. The ER nurses helped to settle him in the car seat as comfortably as possible with a pillow and blankets, water, pain medication, and a urinal and car-sick bag to use if needed.

I made another call to our friends to let them know we were heading out. Of course, they were concerned about my driving alone with Dwight being so sick. But we both knew it was best to get back to Seattle, and this was the best way to do it. I felt confident that Jesus would give me strength for the journey, and He surely did. We drove straight to the VA hospital in Seattle and checked into the ER where, after preliminary testing was done and cancer confirmed, Dwight made his proclamation of "I want to live."

The teams of doctors at the Veterans Administration Medical Center in Seattle are amazing. Most of the doctors we saw at the VA rotate between there, the University of Washington Medical Center, and also the Seattle Cancer Care Alliance. Both of those facilities are renowned for their excellence. I am well aware that VA medical care, in general, has received a bad reputation over the past several years in some parts of the country. But I tell everyone I can about the excellent care Dwight received, and continues to receive, from doctors and nurses and everyone on staff at the Seattle Veterans Medical Center.

Dwight was admitted to the hospital, and the process of determining the exact diagnoses and plan of care began. At times like that, we are so anxious to get answers and for treatment to begin. But I was there all day, every day, and could see the long and careful process that it is to not only diagnose properly but also to coordinate all the various doctors that would be involved in the treatment. I often wished things would move ahead faster, but at the same time, I was so grateful Dwight was in the hospital receiving care and pain control during these important initial days.

Eventually, the diagnosis was named, and it was one that the doctors had most feared. "Stage IV aggressive high-grade B-cell non-Hodgkin's lymphoma, metastatic to liver."

The treatment plan was intensive chemotherapy that would be administered as an in-patient during six sessions, each continuously over a period of five days, with two weeks at home between sessions. A port was inserted into Dwight's chest to be able to administer the drugs directly into Dwight's body without having to use the veins in his arms. The chemo drugs were very strong, and a person is considered "hot" during that intensive treatment. The patient's body fluids: blood, saliva, urine, were actually toxic and could burn the skin of someone else if they came in contact.

Here I want to say something about our decision to agree to such strong chemotherapy. We are aware of people who strongly speak out against such chemotherapy that is actually toxic in itself. And when faced with life and death decisions about health care, each individual needs to make the choices that are best for them. Dwight and I had experienced the use of strong drugs and treatments in 2008 during his fifty-five days in ICU. Treatments that were necessary for his condition at the time and that saved his life. We believe that God has led people in the discovery and the development of these life-saving drugs, chemotherapies to kill cancer, and even the machines used to carry them into the patient's body. We thank God for all of them! We believe God led us in making the choices that were right for us, and we are grateful to Him for everything He did for us along that journey.

Cancer is so prevalent in our society today, and many of you reading this will be painfully familiar with what a patient goes through—and what the caregiver goes through as well—during the weeks or months of intense chemotherapy. So I do not feel to detail a lot of that here. It is a roller coaster of emotions to deal with the physical effects of the treatment. It is also, truthfully, a time when faith and hope are the lifelines you hang on to while also preparing yourself as well as your family for life without you. Dwight and I went through all that as well.

One thing that gave strength to both of us was that, because this was still in the pre-COVID days, I was able to stay with him in the hospital for each of the five-day inpatient sessions. In the cancer ward where patients are receiving chemo, they allow just one person in each room. This is to protect each patient, so they do not need to share the bathroom and so on. So, with only one patient per room, the spouse is able to stay in the room as well if they choose to do that, and other wives of their vet husbands were there the same as I was. Some weeks, I slept in a recliner or sleep chair, but other weeks there was a second hospital bed in the room, so I could use that to sleep very comfortably. It helped both Dwight and me to experience the highs and the lows of each day together, to pray together, and draw strength from each other. A very different experience than I had ten years ago when Dwight was unconscious for most of that long hospital stay and unable to communicate with me.

Our days in the hospital were spent quietly. We would have many short conversations with the nurses when they came in to care for Dwight throughout the day and night, and when the doctors came in, we were eager to hear their expert thoughts or occasional adjustments in the treatment plan. I brought my little travel coffee set-up and the makings for peanut butter and jelly sandwiches for my breakfast and lunch each day; then, for supper, I would go to the cafeteria to buy a salad and bring it to the room to sit by Dwight's bed where we would have dinner together. It encouraged us both to have a comfortable routine to our days, easing the emotion and discomfort of the cancer treatment helping to make it less stressful.

Dwight watched his car restoration shows on television. I read several good Christian novels that my friend Lori had loaned to me, and I spent some long peaceful hours coloring! Another friend, Jann, had bought me a Psalms coloring book for adults, complete with gel pens and colored pencils. What girl doesn't love a new box of crayons! (And these were high-tech coloring tools for sure!)

With Christmas approaching, I decided to embroider dishtowels for our granddaughters and pillowcases for our great-grandchildren. That was also a peaceful and time-consuming way to spend my days.

It was always a highlight when someone came by for a short visit. The Seattle VA hospital is forty miles or more from where most of our friends live, and we appreciated their gift of time and effort to drive all the way through the city to come and see us at the hospital. One day during the first week of chemo treatments, a couple from church, who at the time were still fairly new friends to us, came and gave us a huge dose of encouragement. When Lori and Jay arrived for their visit, Jay gave Dwight a cute little brown teddy bear. An unusual gift for a grown man, but we took it as a sweet gesture. But then Jay told us that a few years before, he had been diagnosed with Stage IV lymphoma that had metastasized to his bone marrow. He had also gone through intense chemo treatments—so both he and

Lori knew exactly what Dwight and I were going through—and Jay had been healed. Today he is still cancer-free.

This news sent shock waves of blessing through both of us. Dwight wept as he realized this friend sitting before him had gone through the same kind of cancer, so he really understood the battle, and he had won. It was another beautiful encouragement that Dwight would win the battle too.

Dwight named that little teddy bear "Pete" (aka Peter, the outspoken disciple of Jesus). Pete sat on the side table during every hospital visit thereafter, "watching to make sure the nurses and doctors did everything right," in addition to starting many conversations that led to prayer.

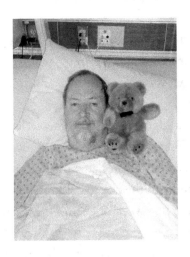

Dwight and "Pete"

Another thing that gave us great strength was the large, faithful—and faith-filled—army of prayer warriors who were praying for both of us. Throughout the months of tests, chemo treatments, and hospitalizations, we were covered in prayer literally 24/7 by networks of prayer in our family, throughout the Aglow family, and our church family. We could both feel the strength of those prayers. They were our lifeline.

Through the ease of the electronic communications we have available to us, each day and sometimes even more than once a day, I would send text messages to my main contact in each of our special family groups. I knew each of them would pass along the praise report or prayer request of the day—or the moment—and prayers filled with understanding would be lifted up to the Father.

It was important to us both that we share enough information with those covering us in prayer that they could pray with understanding of the real-time situation and also that they would pray according to the way we knew God was leading us. Many years ago, when we were still living in Minnesota, a dear man at our church became seriously ill with cancer. Today, great strides have been made in cancer treatments, and thankfully, it is no longer the deadly disease it was in those days. But as Dwight prayed for this man, he felt strongly in his spirit that God had told him this man was not going to die from this cancer. Dwight felt led to fast for his friend for seven days. It was the first time he had fasted for so many days, and it was a struggle for him, but he knew what God had spoken to him, and his faith was great that the man would be healed.

Not long after Dwight's fast ended, sadly, his friend died of that cancer. Dwight cried out to God to help him understand why he had felt so sure of what he heard God spoke to him, but the friend died anyway? God answered in a still, small voice in Dwight's heart, "Whose prayers should I have answered?"

We learned that many people were praying for this man to die quickly and to be out of his suffering. Dwight came to understand through that experience that we should always pray with faith for God to heal and restore. Of course, God is sovereign, and He will do His will and have the final word in all things. His will is what we always want. But how we pray is also important. We wanted our family and friends to surround us with faith-filled prayers of surrender to God, and for His healing and restoring power, and to have full reign in our lives.

Every person in our "prayer army" was amazing and deeply appreciated. But I want to share a bit about the men at our church, Sonrise Christian Center, who lived through this journey with their brother Dwight in a way that I actually consider a supernatural anointing.

For about the past fifteen years, "Man Prayer" has been growing in numbers, strength, and anointing. Every Friday morning, sixty to seventy-plus men gather in the sanctuary at 4:00 a.m., 5:00 a.m., or 6:00 a.m., depending on their work schedules, for an hour of prayer. The first twenty minutes are spent alone in prayer or reading their Bibles. The next twenty minutes is corporate prayer when the men encircle the sanctuary, praying strongly and passionately in turn. In the last twenty minutes, they break into small groups for personal prayer. There is beautiful mentoring and accountability in these small groups as the men have built relationships of trust with one another. They end the time with all the men shouting in unison—as one!—their loud, deep voices nearly shaking the rafters! A couple of times on Father's Day, when our pastor had all the men stand, he had them all do the "As one!" shout, and it moved us all! Wow. There is power in declaration!

I must explain that I know all these things only from what Dwight has told me! It is a time reserved for the men and is very special for them all.

Our dear friend Rob was my prayer contact at church, and he faithfully sent out our praise and prayer reports, staying in touch with me to give us feedback about some of the beautiful prayers that were prayed and the encouraging or prophetic words that had come from the men or others at church. Of course, our pastors were also in close contact with us, and they also were a great part of this network. Dwight was an elder in our church at the time and known and loved by everyone. The men shared with their wives, and they were also part of the prayer army!

There was something more than "just" prayer for Dwight that was happening at our church. People were using the text message updates they were receiving from Rob and interceding strongly for Dwight. And as they were seeing progress and results to their prayers, they began to recognize their prayers were reaching heaven, and they became part of the healing process. They "took ownership," in a good way, for Dwight's slow but steady progress.

In notes I saved from this time, I have some beautiful examples of this. In December 2018, I had sent a text to Rob with news of the results of a CT scan that had been done mid-way through the chemo treatment weeks. He had undergone three week-long treatments and had three more scheduled. The CT scan showed a definite decrease in the cancer. We were able to tell him the cancer is disappearing fast!

Rob's response was amazing. He said, "I have received more responses to my forward of this news than to any other email I can recall. I'm telling you, this has not been about Dwight only, but about testing the body (of Christ), measuring our response, our faith, our readiness to back one of our own… I believe we are going to see a turn in the overall battle against cancer. If Sonrise is to be a cancer-free zone, as some have spoken in the name of the Lord, we expect to find the tide of battle reversing. I am greatly encouraged for you two and for the body of Christ. Many have prayed, as we have, that the Lord would use you to bring healing to others. Truly, what the enemy intended for your harm, the Lord will use for your benefit, and others will also benefit from your victory."

Not long after that, in January of 2019, Rob said in a text of encouragement to us, "The body of Christ is represented by our physical bodies. Just as we have an immune system to fight infection and other systems working together to accomplish healing when there is injury, the saints of God go to battle immediately for the aid of one in need. It's one of the most awesome sights I have ever witnessed, truly breathtaking in grace and beauty! People are praying consistently. I'll send the update in the morning before Man Prayer, and we will join as one for Dwight. There is a shared, strong sense that this is not only for Dwight, but that if we press in, the tide will turn for many." That strong sense to press in to pray continues until today.

At one point in a text I sent to Rob, I expressed that I felt bad to be sending such a constant stream of prayer requests, knowing so many others need prayer too. His response to me was so uplifting. I want to share this for others who may hold back from sharing their prayer requests, thinking other people's needs are greater or more important.

Rob told me, "There are many (prayer needs), but as they say in "lay parables," the squeaky wheel gets the grease. Jesus said to whoever asks it will be given. James says we receive not because we ask not. Don't give up asking! Be bold! Some are too shy, and we try to speak up for them, but I feel very strongly that updates are critical to "dialing in" our prayer. It's a little like making a radio call for artillery support. Follow-up communication to inform the shooters about the effectiveness of the barrage and to adjust their fire can make the difference between bringing down strongholds and shelling the sea!"

Dwight and I in the hospital during one of his chemo weeks

During the months of chemo treatments, Dwight was one week in hospital and two weeks at home, recuperating and gaining strength for the next round. Of course, he had to be careful because his immune system was depleted by the chemo, and often he had no strength to leave our home. But whenever a

Sunday came, and he felt up to it, he wanted to go to church. Thankfully, this was long before the COVID-19 pandemic! He wanted to see his friends who were giving so much to intercede for him, and he wanted them to see him, too. He wanted them to know he was alive and he was still fighting!

He didn't have the strength to stand during praise and worship time, but he was there in body and spirit, and his friends all came to him with happy greetings and well wishes. Sometimes, he felt strong enough to join the prayer team at the front of the sanctuary at the end of the service to pray for people. His body was weak, but the Holy Spirit still worked strongly through his prayers. It meant a lot for everyone to see him in church, and so many told us how they were also being strengthened to see him.

One week, the chemo treatment was finished by Saturday night, so Dwight convinced the doctors to discharge him on Sunday morning so he could go to church. We drove from the hospital straight to church and slipped into the service just after the message had begun, and sat in the back row. Pastor Dan stopped his message and greeted him, and after service, all the men gathered around where we were seated to pray for Dwight. There were not many dry eyes in the house.

Two times we were to report to the hospital on a Friday morning, so I drove Dwight to the church to participate in Man Prayer before going on to the hospital. I sat in the church lobby with a book and felt the Spirit of God as those powerful men prayed and stormed heaven for all the needs of the day—including for Dwight. They were all so happy to have him in their midst.

God lets *nothing* be wasted. Whatever you might be struggling with, others are likely also being affected in some way or another. God is working in your life, in their lives, in the situation that in some way affects you all. It is His heart to always work things for your good and for His Glory. God is a loving Father, and you are His favorite child! Run to Him with every thought, every need.

Of course, Dwight was in the hospital for cancer treatment, a serious matter for sure, but God never lets even our time be wasted when our hearts are tuned to Him. One of the precious things that happened during those week-long hospital stays were the conversations he had with many of the nurses about the Lord and the opportunities Dwight was given to pray for them.

Nurses are an amazing "breed" of people. Deeply caring, exceptionally intelligent, fearless, and bold. But they are also just people, with illness in their own families, problems in their marriages, or troubles with their children. When they discovered Dwight was a believer (something he easily found ways to tell each of them), they would often take a moment to tell him about their lives and would always eagerly accept prayer. Many times there were brief but precious moments in prayer spent with one of the nurses, men and women alike, who had come to know Dwight as a man to be trusted with their prayer request. And those times certainly gave a new level of meaning to what Dwight was going through in the treatments he was receiving.

Sometimes when we go back to the VA for routine checkups, we take a few minutes to go up to the cancer ward to say hi to the nurses on duty, and often they are ones who had cared for Dwight. On one of those short visits, the pretty young woman named Mindy came around the counter to give Dwight a hug. She said she had just been thinking about him and the prayer he had prayed for her and her family—what a blessing for us both.

Precious memories also are the times Dwight was able to pray for the doctors caring for him. He knew their time was extremely valuable, so he could not detain them for long. It was amazing to watch their faces as Dwight told them he was praying for them because God was using them to bring healing to his body. They looked at him, usually with small, amazed smiles on their faces before they turned to leave the room.

The chemo was rough, but it killed the cancer! He finished his last treatment in February 2019, and at his follow-up appointment a few months later, the PET scan showed no cancer. The doctors hesitate to use the term "cancer-free," and they reminded us that lymphoma is a cyclical disease and reoccurrences are common. That may be, but we have seen God work in some very "uncommon" ways, and my prayer is that God will "break the cycle" of lymphoma in Dwight's body. I also pray that when God calls us both to our heavenly home, it will not be a disease but just old age that ends our days. Lord, may it be so. Amen.

As I write this, Dwight is outside puttering with something in the garage. He tires out more quickly than he would like, but life is good, and we give all praise and thanks to Jesus—our ever-present help.

Thoughts to ponder

- Has God spoken promises to your heart that you are still waiting to see come into reality for your life?
- Is there an area in your life where you need to believe God's promise to you more than what you see with your eyes?

With Confident Hope We Journey Forward

> Therefore, we who have fled to him for refuge can have great confidence as we hold to the hope that is before us. This hope is a strong and trustworthy anchor for our souls. It leads us through the curtain into God's inner sanctuary.
>
> Hebrews 6:18-19 (NLT)

Thank you for choosing to read this book. I sincerely hope you have found it to be much more than "a story of a lot of things that have happened to one family."

In several places in scripture, we are told to testify, to tell others what God has done. I have been strengthened by reading the testimony of others, and my fervent prayer is that you have been strengthened in your own journey by reading this testimony of what God has done for me and my husband.

Whatever He has done for us, He will surely do for you also. His love for you knows no bounds. The scripture above is from the book of Hebrews, a book in the Bible that tells us who Jesus was as a Son and what He does for us. I encourage you to read the words of Hebrews for yourself and let God speak into your own life through those loving words of encouragement.

I want to repeat a prayer of my heart from the prologue at the beginning of this book. I shared that my greatest hope is that I can reach out to you who are battling life's circumstances. There may be events in your life that took place years ago, but the struggle is still very real, or events that you are walking through right now, and you are weary and wonder how you can go on. I pray that through my testimony of God's sustaining strength, love, and courage, you might discover—or re-discover—His strength on the inside of you.

⁂

A few years ago, I was invited to speak at an Aglow retreat in Alaska. We were in a beautiful Christian camp deep in the forest, and I thoroughly enjoyed the rustic cabins and surroundings. The camp was along the banks of a lake and, even though there was still ice on the water, we held a baptism for several brave women who wanted to get baptized then and there! (Thankfully, I was not asked to go into the water and do the dunking!)

I was asked to speak three times, and the theme of the retreat led me to share about overcoming struggles in my life. I found myself sharing about my struggle with alcohol and how, years before, on the night of my salvation experience, God had lifted that desire/need from my life. But that was not the final end of that battle. Remember, the enemy of our souls, who is Satan, is always looking for ways to kill, steal, and destroy. And every struggle with him is nasty. But never forget that our God is greater!

At that Alaska retreat, I shared how, many years after finding freedom from alcohol, even after I had become a leader in Christian ministry and was living my life in the best way I could to glorify God, that old enemy began to harass me. Satan is so hateful and will stoop to any level to try and bring destruction to our lives.

A season of great temptation entered my life. I was suddenly struggling with that old desire, remembering the old feelings of carefree oblivion and a feeling of just throwing everything away to succumb to my old way of life. Alcoholism had deeply affected my immediate family, including my grandfather, my father, and my sister. My dear sister, three years younger than I, died at age fifty-seven from complications that alcoholism had caused. The roots inside of me were buried deep, but Satan knew they were still there.

What! That's absurd, you might be saying! No, it was very, very real. And I was shocked that I could be tempted so viciously.

At that Alaska Aglow retreat, I knew God wanted me to bare my heart about that struggle. I told the women that I felt certain there were others in our midst who were struggling with such an enemy. It might be alcohol or something else that had taken control of their lives. I shared they might be sitting there at this retreat, dressed in their nice clothes with their hair and make-up just so, saying all the right things. But they knew the depth of their secret struggle. And they were not always winning the battle. The shame they were hiding had become too much to bear.

As I spoke, I heard a few women in the audience begin to cry quietly. And as I continued, wails began to come from all over the auditorium. Sounds of deep, heart-wrenching weeping rose up as women found the courage to admit in their hearts, to God, what they had been trying to fight against all by themselves.

The Aglow Area Team and I prayed for people until the wee hours of the morning. Even the women who were embarrassed to come forward for prayer at first, not wanting others to know of their struggle, found the courage to hope they might find freedom too. It was beautiful to watch women step forward filled with expectation and into the freedom that our loving and accepting Jesus has for every one of us. I weep as I remember all the emotions of that night and the freedoms that Jesus sealed in many lives.

We all need hope to get through the battles that we are called to navigate in our lives. At times in our journey, we rejoice in the victory, but at other times hanging on to hope is our only comfort. At those times, we hang on to scriptures such as this one in Romans 12:12 "Rejoice in our confident hope. Be patient in trouble, and keep on praying" (NLT).

In the pages of this book, I have tried to be as honest as I could be in sharing my heart and emotions through each part of the journey that Dwight and I have traveled together since 1970. Everything that has happened to one of us, both of us experienced from our own perspective. And together, we have learned to rest in and rely on God's peace and His presence in all circumstances.

A chapter not yet written is that of the diagnosis of Parkinson's disease Dwight received in October of 2020. This is also being attributed to exposure to Agent Orange while serving in the military. When we received this news, we both felt scared, especially as we began to educate ourselves about the devastating effects of this disease. That night, after we had received the diagnosis, alone with God, I opened my heart to Him and confessed that I didn't feel I had the energy to fight another battle. I felt depleted, with no strength left. Even while I was still confessing this to Jesus, I "heard" Him speak to my heart. Over and over, He said, "I will fight for you."

Later I found His promise in Exodus 14:14 "The Lord himself will fight for you. Just stay calm" (NLT).

Oh Lord, how can we ever say thanks for all You have done for us!

⁂

Several years ago, as I sat in the backyard swing that Dwight built for me—my favorite place in all the world—I asked God, "What have I really learned from You through all of the things I've gone through in my life?" He spoke these words to my heart. I encourage you, dear reader, to take these words for yourself as well. Jesus said;

> *I am with you always—ready for you to lift unto Me the devastation of your soul, the weight of your grief, the sorrow you carry in your heart.*
> *Let Me carry it for you.*
> *Empty yourself of these things that weigh you down.*
> *Give them to Me and fill yourself instead with My love.*
> *In My love, you will find rest and peace.*

My friend, God did not cause all the things that have happened in your life. But He was there through every one of them. The "why" question may remain unanswered. But there is no question about the love of Jesus and His presence as we go through the trials and battles in our lives.

And in today's world, when global pandemics are the overwhelming news literally around the world, for us as believers, the need for hope is greater than ever. This is confirmed in 1 Timothy 4:10 (NLT): "This is why we work hard and continue to struggle, for our hope is in the living God, who is the Savior of all people and particularly of all believers."

May you find renewed and confident hope through whatever circumstance your journey is taking you. God's gifts of strength and hope will sustain you to allow you to persevere through your own challenges and personal battles to God's perfect peace.

"I cried to the Lord with my voice, and He heard me from His holy hill. Selah" (Psalm 3:4, NKJV).

Thoughts to ponder

- Are there secret struggles in your life that you have not yet faced?
- Do you know, really know, that God loves you even now and is longing to release you from the hold of these struggles?
- Is the "old man" in your life dead but not yet "resting in peace"?
- Are you ready to release it all to Jesus and "just stay calm"?

ABOUT THE AUTHOR

Dwight & Jervae, Christmas 2019

Until her retirement in December 2021 Jervae served as Executive Director of the Global Field Office at the headquarter offices of Aglow International, where she had been on staff since 1980. She traveled extensively for Aglow and enjoyed building relationships with Aglow leaders around the world.

She shares a powerful story of God's redemption. After tragedies and losses, God has ministered joy and wholeness back into Jervae's life, and she continues to share that wonderful message of God's restorative love and power whenever she can.

Dwight loves the outdoors and approaches life with humor and gusto. Through deep emotional healing that he has found in his own life, God has placed within him a "father's heart" anointing and a strong desire to minister hope and wholeness to men while helping them discover and pursue their destiny. Currently,

Dwight serves on the prayer ministry team at Sonrise Christian Center in Everett, Washington.

Their family has grown to include nine grandchildren and thirteen great-grandchildren. Their quiver is full, and each child is a beautiful blessing.

Jervae and Dwight make their home in Tulalip, Washington, about forty miles north of Seattle. "A little house on an acre of land surrounded by old-growth cedar trees."

Jervae can be contacted at jervaebrooks@gmail.com

PHOTO LIST

CPSIA information can be obtained
at www.ICGtesting.com
Printed in the USA
BVHW040917110122
625980BV00013B/290